The Nugget Finders

He struck, and lo! a yellow streak became plainly visible. "Boys, ... I believe we've found a nugget."—*Chap. XI.*

The Nugget Finders

A Tale of the Gold Fields of Australia

By H. Alger

CONTENTS

CHAP.

I. PLANNING FOR THE FUTURE

II. A TIMELY RESCUE

III. STARTING FOR THE MINES

IV. A VICTIM OF TREACHERY

V. A DISAGREEABLE SURPRISE

VI. FLETCHER TURNS UP AGAIN

VII. A TRIAL AND ITS TRAGIC FINALE

VIII. LOST IN THE WOODS

IX. A DANGEROUS ACQUAINTANCE

X. THE BOYS ARRIVE AT BENDIGO

XI. STRIKING LUCK

XII. THE NUGGET IN DANGER

XIII. A THIEF'S EMBARRASSMENT

XIV. BAFFLED CUPIDITY

XV. SELLING THE CLAIM

XVI. TAKEN CAPTIVE

XVII. FAREWELL TO MELBOURNE

XVIII. A HEART-BROKEN RELATIVE

XIX. HOME AGAIN

XX. THE BOYS SECURE POSITIONS

XXI. CONCLUSION

THE NUGGET FINDERS

CHAPTER I
PLANNING FOR THE FUTURE

 A STOUT gentleman of middle age and two boys were sitting in the public room of a modest inn in Melbourne. The gentleman was known to the public as Professor Hemmenway, who announced himself on the programme of his entertainment as "The Magician of Madagascar," though he freely confessed to his confidential friends that he had never seen the island of that name.

The two boys were Harry Vane and Jack Pendleton, boys of sixteen. One had come to Australia as assistant to the professor, and had been accustomed to sing one or two popular songs at the magical entertainments which he gave, besides rendering himself generally useful. Jack Pendleton was a young sailor, who had resolved to try his fortune in the new country, either at the mines or in any other employment offering fair compensation, before resuming his profession. Harry and the professor had been passengers on board Jack's ship, and the two boys had struck up an enduring friendship. The ship had been wrecked, and they had spent some weeks together on an uninhabited island, from which they were finally rescued. It had been the professor's intention to give a series of performances in Melbourne and other parts of Australia, but the unexpected delay had led him to change his plans, and he now proposed to return home at once. Harry

Vane, however, having no near family ties, for he was an orphan, felt inclined to stay with Jack, and try his fortune for a time in the New World, which appealed strongly to his imagination and youthful love of adventure. The day had arrived for the professor's departure, and he and the two boys were waiting for the lighter to take him down the Yarra Yarra River to the point of embarkation, eight miles distant.

"Harry," said the professor kindly, "I don't like to leave you here. You are only sixteen, and I feel that it is a great undertaking for you to attempt to make a living so many thousand miles from your native land. I shall feel anxious about you."

"I don't feel anxious about myself, professor," said Harry, with the confidence natural to youth. "I am young and strong, and I mean to succeed."

"But suppose you fall sick?"

"Then Jack will look out for me."

"You may be sure of that, Harry," said the young sailor, with a glance of affection at Harry.

"You might both fall sick."

"Is it best to borrow trouble?" said Harry, smiling. "I think we shall come out all right. But I am sorry you won't stay with us, professor."

Professor Hemmenway shook his head.

"I am three times your age, Harry," he said, "and am not as hopeful or sanguine as you. Besides, I have a wife and children at home who are already very anxious at my long silence; I did indeed mean to make a professional tour of Australia, but the shipwreck and those lonely weeks on the island changed my plans. I have a competence already, and can make an income at home twice as large as my expenses. Why should I incur any risks?"

"I don't know but you are right, professor, but Jack and I are not so fortunate. Neither of us has a competence, and our prospects are probably better here than at home."

"Remember, Harry, that if you return I shall be glad to continue your engagement and will even increase your salary."

Jack Pendleton fixed his eyes anxiously on Harry's face. He feared that he would yield to the professor's persuasion and leave him, but his anxiety was soon removed.

"Thank you, professor," said Harry, "but I don't want to leave Jack. If I return in bad luck, I may look you up and see whether the offer still holds good."

"Do so. You will always find a friend in me. But that reminds me, Harry, of an important consideration. If you are to remain here, you will want some money."

"I have twelve pounds which I have saved up in your service."

"And how much have you, Jack?"

The young sailor coloured, and looked a little uneasy.

"I have only two pounds," he answered.

"That is, we have fourteen pounds between us, Jack," said Harry promptly.

"That is too little," said the professor, shaking his head. "You must let me be your banker."

"On one condition, professor, with thanks for your kindness."

"What is that?"

"A gentleman at home, Mr. Thomas Conway, has charge of fifty pounds belonging to me. I was fortunate enough to save a railway train from destruction, and this is the money the passengers raised for me. I will give you an order on him for the amount of your loan."

"That is unnecessary, Harry; I am willing to wait till you return."

"Something might happen to me, professor, and I shall feel more comfortable to think that my debts are paid."

"Have your own way, then, Harry. Shall I give you the whole amount?"

"No, professor, I am afraid it would make me less enterprising."

"How much shall it be?"

"Jack and I have fourteen pounds between us. Twenty more ought to be sufficient."

"As you please, Harry; but if you get into trouble, promise to communicate with me, and send for assistance."

"I will, sir."

At this moment a carriage drew up in front of the inn.

"It is the carriage I ordered to take me to the lighter," said the professor. "You and Jack must go with me to the ship and see the last of me."

"With great pleasure, sir. Come along, Jack."

The driver put the professor's trunk on the carriage, and they set out. It was a new trunk, bought in Melbourne, for the professor's trunk and clothing had been lost at the time of the shipwreck. His first care had been to get a complete outfit in

Melbourne, and he was now as well provided as when he left home.

The two boys found the trip down the river a pleasant one. The trip by land would have been considerably shorter, but the professor preferred the river. The distance to the mouth is nine miles. The city of Melbourne is situated chiefly on the north bank, and is a handsomely built and prosperous town. The country bordering the river is not particularly inviting, but it was new, and the two boys regarded it with interest. The soil was barren and sandy, and the trees, which were numerous, were eucalyptus or gum trees, which do not require a rich soil, but grow with great rapidity on sterile soil.

Harry could not help feeling sad as he bade farewell to his good friend the professor.

"I have only you now, Jack," he said. "I don't know what lies before us, but we must stick fast to each other in sunshine and in storm."

Jack's only answer was to seize Harry's hand and press it warmly. Nothing more was needed.

The two boys returned to the Crown Hotel in time for dinner, of which they partook with the zest to be expected of boys thoroughly healthy. When the meal was over they repaired to the public room.

"Now, Jack," said Harry, "it is necessary for us to settle on our plans."

"All right," said Jack.

"Have you anything to propose?"

"No, Harry, you are smarter than I am, and I leave it to you."

"Thank you, Jack, for your confidence, but we are on a par here. Neither of us knows much about Australia. We have a great deal to learn."

"Then you had better decide for us both."

"Very well, I accept the responsibility, but I prefer to talk over my plans with you. First of all, then, shall we stay in Melbourne, or strike for the mines?"

"Just as you say, Harry, but I would prefer the mines."

"I feel that way myself, and for that reason I have been making some inquiries. There are three principal localities—Ballarat, Bendigo, and Ovens. We might try one of the three, and if we don't have good luck make our way to another."

"Which shall we try first?"

"I have thought of Bendigo. I hear of one party that cleared two thousand pounds out of one hole."

"How much is that?" asked Jack, who was not very well acquainted with any but United States currency.

"It is equal to ten thousand dollars," answered Harry.

"That's a big pile of money," said Jack, his eyes sparkling.

"True, but we mustn't expect to be so fortunate. It isn't everybody who succeeds as well as that."

"I should be satisfied with a thousand, Harry."

"And what would you do with it, Jack?"

"Convey it home to my mother, Harry. But I would fix it so that my stepfather couldn't get hold of it."

"You are a good boy, Jack, for thinking so much of your mother. I wish I had a mother to provide for," and Harry Vane looked sober.

"Do you know how far off Bendigo is, Harry?"

"About a hundred miles. That is, it is seventy-five miles to Mount Alexander, and the mines are twenty-five miles to the north of that."

"It won't take us long to travel a hundred miles," said Jack hopefully.

"On the contrary, it will be a long and difficult journey, as far as I can find out. The country is full of bogs, swamps, and moist land."

"Then we can't walk?"

"No; the custom is to charter a cart, drawn by oxen, which will give a chance to carry a stock of provisions. The roads are not very well marked, and are often impassable."

This description rather discouraged Jack, who was more used to the sea and its dangers than to land travel.

"I wish we could go by water," he said.

"So do I, Jack, but unfortunately Bendigo happens to be inland. However, you've got good stout legs, and can get along as well as the thousands that do go. Besides, it will give us a fine chance to see the country."

"Ye-es," said Jack doubtfully, for he had very little of the traveller's curiosity that prompts so many to visit strange lands.

"There's another difficulty besides the mud," continued Harry thoughtfully.

"What's that?"

"The bushrangers."

"Who are they?"

"Haven't you heard of them?" asked Harry in surprise.

"I heard two men speaking of them last night, but I didn't take much notice."

"They are highwaymen—robbers, who wander about and attack parties of miners and travellers, and unless successfully resisted, strip them of all their property."

"Are we likely to meet them?" said Jack eagerly.

"I hope not; but we stand a chance of doing so."

"When are we going to start?" asked Jack with alacrity.

"Do you want to meet these gentlemen, Jack?" inquired Harry with a smile.

"There'll be some fun about it," responded Jack.

Harry shrugged his shoulders.

"I don't think there'll be much fun about being robbed," he said. "I would rather they would give us a wide berth, for my part."

Jack did not answer, but from that time he was eager to set out for the mines. The hint of danger invested the journey with a charm it had not hitherto possessed in his eyes.

While the boys were conversing, a tall man, with heavy black whiskers and wearing a rough suit and a slouch hat, appeared to listen attentively. At this point he rose from his seat, and lounged over to where Harry and Jack were seated.

"Young gentlemen," he said, "do I understand that you are thinking of going to the mines?"

"Yes, sir," answered Harry, surveying his inquirer with some attention.

"And you talk of going to Bendigo?"

"Yes; do you know anything about the place?"

"I ought to. I only came from there last month."

"What luck did you have there, may I ask?"

"Pretty fair. I brought back about a hundred and fifty pounds in gold-dust."

"And how long were you there?"

"Four weeks."

"That is pretty good pay for the time."

"That's so, especially as I made little or nothing the first three weeks. I struck it rich the last week."

"What do you say to that, Jack?" said Harry, turning to his companion.

"That pays better than being a sailor," answered Jack, smiling.

"I should say it did."

"When do you expect to start?" asked the stranger.

"As soon as we can get ready," Harry replied.

"You are right there. Have you got money?"

"Why?" asked Harry, rather suspiciously.

"It will cost something for an outfit."

"Yes; we have a moderate sum with us."

"That is well," said the stranger approvingly. "Do you know," he continued meditatively, "I have a great mind to go with you?"

"Then you are not satisfied with your pile?" said Harry.

"There's very little left of it," said their new acquaintance.

"You haven't spent a hundred and fifty pounds in a month?" said Harry, in surprise.

"Pretty much. I may have twenty pounds left."

"You must have been living high, then."

"No. I have lived plainly, but the faro table has taken most of it. I'm so near broke that I may as well go back to the mines for a fresh supply before my money is all gone."

"We shall be glad of your company, sir."

"My name is Fletcher—Dick Fletcher my friends call me."

"I am Harry Vane, and my friend is Jack Pendleton."

"We will drink to our better acquaintance. Here, John," addressing the bar-keeper, "three glasses of ale here."

"If you won't mind, Jack and I will take lemonade."

Fletcher stared at them in amazement.

"You don't drink ale?" he said.

"We belong to the temperance society," said Harry, smiling.

"You won't keep that up long at the mines," said Fletcher, shrugging his shoulders.

Harry did not reply, but quietly resolved that he would disprove that statement.

CHAPTER II
A TIMELY RESCUE

NE circumstance led Harry to hurry his intended departure. He found to his dismay that the hotel charge for their very plain accommodations was a pound a day for each of them. But Melbourne was full of strangers, drawn thither by flaming accounts of the richness of the mines and the bright prospects of acquiring sudden fortunes, and war prices were prevalent everywhere.

"A pound a day!" exclaimed Jack in open-eyed amazement. "Do they take us for millionaires?"

"I began to think they were imposing upon us," said Harry, "till I made inquiries elsewhere. I find a pound a day is about the usual tariff for such accommodations as we have."

"But we have only a small bedroom, and the meals are very common."

"That is true, but it seems to make no difference."

"Our money will soon be gone at that rate," said Jack soberly. "Mine is already gone."

"No, it isn't, Jack. We are going to share and share alike, you know."

"But that is imposing on you, Harry," protested the young sailor earnestly.

"Let me judge of that, Jack; I'd a good deal rather have your company and half of the money than be alone and have the whole."

"Thank you, Harry. You are a true friend. I can't do much for you, but I'll do what I can."

"If I had known of the high prices, I would have drawn more money from the professor," continued Harry. "However, I can make this do. But I want to start to-morrow, if possible. We shall then be owing four days' board each, and that will make eight pounds."

At this point Fletcher joined them.

"By the way," said he nonchalantly, "I want to ask a little favour."

"What is it?" asked Harry unsuspiciously.

"I am rather short of money. Can you lend me five pounds?"

"I am sorry to refuse, Mr. Fletcher," he said, "but Jack and I are ourselves very poorly provided with money, and just before you came in we were considering how we could manage to pay for the necessary outfit."

"Haven't you got five pounds?" asked Fletcher quickly.

"Of course we have, or we should be unable to get to the mines."

"Then I think you might oblige me," he continued, looking very much displeased.

"I am the best judge of my circumstances," said Harry shortly.

Fletcher looked hard at him, and saw that the boy he had to deal with had a mind of his own, and was not to be imposed upon easily. Still he made a further effort.

"Then I think," he said coldly, "I shall not be able to assist you in your preparations."

"Just as you please," answered Harry promptly. "As you volunteered, I accepted your proposal. Now I will act for myself. I have heard of a party about to start, and I will arrange to join it."

Fletcher felt that he was outgeneralled. He did not mean to let Harry and Jack slip through his fingers, for he had an idea, notwithstanding Harry's disclaimer, that he had a large sum of money, and thought he would be a good party to hang on to. He saw that he had made a false move, and hastened to repair it.

"Excuse me," he said, assuming a hearty tone; "I was hasty, and I apologise. You are right, and I like you too well to cut up rough, just because you can't do me a favour. There, take my hand, and we will make it all up."

"With pleasure," answered Harry, as he accepted the proffered hand, and Jack followed his example. Nevertheless, Fletcher's demand had produced an unpleasant effect upon him. The coarse-grained selfishness of the man had shown through his outward varnish of good-fellowship, and he felt that henceforth he must be on his guard.

"I may have to ask for some money, however," continued Fletcher, in an offhand manner, "for it is necessary to buy supplies for our journey. You know we shan't be able to put up at hotels on our way, but must furnish our own meals."

"So I have heard," answered Harry. "What is it customary to take?"

"Well, it will be best to buy a bag of coffee, a sack of flour, some ship biscuits, potatoes, and sugar. That will do to start on, and we shall vary our diet by what we are able to kill on the way."

"What can we kill?"

"Well, kangaroo meat isn't bad, and we can bring down a few birds occasionally."

"Then we shall need guns?"

"Yes, it will be well to have them."

This was another expense upon which Harry had not calculated. He began to think that he had been very improvident. The professor would readily have left him twenty pounds more, and as it would have been repaid with his own money, he was sorry he had not availed himself of it.

"How much do you think the supplies will cost?" asked Harry.

"Well, you had better let me have ten pounds. I think that will be sufficient."

"For the whole or for our share?" asked Harry pointedly.

"For your share," answered Fletcher, after a pause. "It seems to me you are very suspicious."

Really he had intended to make the two boys pay for the whole stock of provisions and save his own purse, for he had in reality as much money as they.

"I only wanted to understand clearly," said Harry quietly. "As we are in some sort partners, that is fair, is it not?"

"Oh, yes," returned Fletcher, but he did not respond with any alacrity. "I'm always fair and aboveboard, I am. No man can say that Dick Fletcher ever tried to get the best of him. Why, if I was better fixed I wouldn't let you two boys pay at all. I'd shoulder the whole thing myself."

"Your offer is a very kind one, Mr. Fletcher——"

"Don't say Mr. Fletcher; call me Dick," interrupted their new acquaintance.

"I will if you wish it, though as you are so much older, it hardly seems proper. What I was going to say was that Jack and myself are determined to pay our share. We couldn't accept any such favour as you mention."

"Now, if you let me have the ten pounds I'll take all the trouble off your hands, and have everything ready for a start to-morrow morning."

"I would prefer to go with you and help select the articles."

Fletcher looked disconcerted.

"Oh, well, if you think I ain't capable——" he began.

"I think nothing of the kind, but I want to learn as much as I can. I may have to do it alone some time."

It was well Harry adhered to his determination. It saved him three pounds, and Fletcher was forced to pay his share, as he had not intended to do. While they were making purchases they were accosted by a tall loose-jointed man, whom it was easy to recognise as a Yankee.

"Goin' to the mines, boys?" he asked in a strong nasal tone.

"Yes," answered Harry.

"So am I. I'd like to hook on to your party if you ain't no objections."

For some reason Dick Fletcher did not appear to relish the proposal.

"I don't think we can accommodate you," he said abruptly.

"I think we can," said Harry, who was beginning to be distrustful of Fletcher, and felt safer in adding another to the party. "There are but three of us, and we shall be glad of your company."

Dick Fletcher looked angry, but did not venture to oppose the plan further.

On the last evening spent in Melbourne the boys decided to take a farewell walk about the city, not knowing when it would again be their fortune to see it. Neither Fletcher nor their new Yankee acquaintance was at hand, and they started by themselves. They did not confine themselves to the more frequented streets, but followed wherever fancy led.

They had no thought of an adventure, but one awaited them.

As they were turning the corner of a narrow street, their attention was suddenly excited by a sharp cry of blended surprise and fright.

"What is it, Jack?" asked Harry, grasping his companion by the arm.

He did not need to await a reply, for by the indistinct light he saw two men struggling a short distance farther on. One appeared to be an old man, with white hair, the other was a man of middle age. Clearly it was a case of attempted robbery.

"Run, Jack, run!" said Harry, in excitement. "Let us help the old man!"

"I'm with you," answered the young sailor briefly.

Harry had in his hand a heavy walking-stick—his only weapon—but he did not stop to consider the personal risk he was running. As he drew near, the old man, whose feeble strength was quite unequal to a conflict with a man so much younger, swayed and fell backward. His assailant bent over him, and despite his feeble resistance began to search his pockets, at the same time indulging in savage threats. The old man gave himself up for lost, but help was nearer than he anticipated.

So occupied was the villain with his disgraceful work that he did not hear the approaching footsteps.

His first intimation of them came in a sounding blow over his shoulders, given by Harry's stick, which was laid on with a good will.

He jumped to his feet with an oath, and darted a rapid glance at his two assailants. Then, much to the surprise of Harry, he turned and ran rapidly away. It was a piece of great good luck, Harry thought, for he was not at all sure that he and Jack combined would have been a match for the highwayman.

"Are you hurt, sir?" asked Harry, bending over the old man.

"Not seriously," was the reply. "Will you kindly help me up?"

With Jack's help Harry got the old man on his feet. He was a tall man, of splendid aspect, over sixty years of age. He looked like a gentleman of wealth and position.

"You have had a narrow escape, sir," said our hero.

"Yes, indeed," answered the old man, "thanks to your brave interference. It surprises me that my brutal assailant should have run away from two boys."

"I am surprised also, sir. I feared we should have a hard fight. I suppose his object was robbery."

"Yes, he must have heard in some way that I had a large sum of money about me. Thanks to you, it is safe."

"I am very glad, sir."

"Do you mind accompanying me to my house? This attack has made me timid."

"With pleasure, sir."

The old gentleman lived perhaps a quarter of a mile distant in a handsome house. He pressed the boys to enter, and they did so. He questioned them as to their plans, and then selecting two bank-notes, urged the boys to accept them as a recognition of the help they had given him at a critical moment. The boys, however, declined positively to accept any compensation, but expressed their satisfaction at having been of service.

"At least," said the old gentleman, "you must promise to call on me when you return from the mines. There is my card."

"That we will do with pleasure, sir," answered Harry.

He looked at the card, and read the name of Henry A. Woolson.

"Harry," said Jack, as they resumed their walk, "do you know that robber had a look like Fletcher?"

"So I thought, Jack, but I had only a glimpse, and could not be sure. I wish he were not to be in our party."

"We must be on our guard; I don't fancy him much."

When the boys saw Fletcher in the morning he appeared as usual, and they were disposed to think they were mistaken. Yet the lurking suspicion occurred to them from time to time, and made them feel uneasy.

The next day they set out on their journey, accompanied by Dick Fletcher and Obed Stackpole.

CHAPTER III
STARTING FOR THE MINES

ARRY may be considered rash in his immediate acceptance of his Yankee acquaintance as a member of their party, but there are some men who need no letters of recommendation. Obed Stackpole certainly was not a handsome man. He was tall, lean, gaunt in figure, with a shambling walk, and his skin was tough and leathery; but in spite of all there was an honest, manly expression which instantly inspired confidence. Both Harry and Jack liked him, but Dick Fletcher seemed to regard him with instinctive dislike.

"What made you accept that scarecrow into our company?" he asked, when Stackpole had left them to make his own arrangements for leaving the city.

Harry smiled.

"He isn't a handsome man," he replied, "but I think he will prove a valuable companion."

"You took no notice of my objection to him," said Fletcher, frowning.

"Our company was too small," returned Harry. "From inquiry I find that parties seldom consist of less than half-a-dozen."

"I know all about that," said Fletcher impatiently. "You might have been guided by me."

"I shall be to some extent," answered Harry, "but not implicitly."

"I am going to have trouble with that boy," thought Fletcher. "Wait till we get on the road." Aloud he said: "If you had mentioned the matter to me I would have found some one to go with us. You had better tell this Yankee that we haven't room for him, and I will do it now."

Fletcher's persistence only aroused vague suspicions in Harry's breast. He felt glad that Stackpole was neither a friend nor likely to prove a confederate of Dick Fletcher, and was resolved to hold on to him.

"I have invited him, and I won't take back the invitation," he said.

"How old are you?" asked Fletcher abruptly.

"Sixteen."

"I should think you were sixty by the tone you assume," said Fletcher with a sneer.

"Do I understand, Mr. Fletcher," asked Harry steadily, "that you claim to control our party?"

"Seeing that I am more than twice as old as you are, I am the natural head of the expedition."

"I cannot admit any such claim. If you are not satisfied to be simply a member of the party, like the rest of us, I shall not be offended if you back out even now."

This, however, did not suit Fletcher, and with a forced laugh he answered, "You are a strange boy, Vane. I don't want to back out, as you term it. I fancy we shall get along together."

"I wish he had decided to leave us," said Harry, when the two boys were alone. "Somehow I distrust him."

"I don't like him myself," said Jack, "but I don't see what harm he can do us."

"Nor I, but I feel safer with this Yankee addition to our party."

About ten o'clock the next morning the little party got off. It is needless to say that Obed Stackpole contributed his full share of expense, and more too, for he furnished the yoke of oxen that were to draw the cart which conveyed their provisions and other outfit.

"I don't want to push in where I ain't wanted," he said, "but I'm used to oxen, and if you want me to, I'll drive these critters, and you three can foller along as you please."

"That'll suit me," said Fletcher, with unusual graciousness. "I've no doubt you understand the business better than I do."

"I ought to understand it," said Stackpole. "I was raised on a farm in New Hampshire, and used to drive oxen when I wasn't tall enough to see over their backs. I never thought then that I'd be drivin' a team in Australy."

"What led you to come out here, Mr. Stackpole?" asked Harry.

"Well, a kinder rovin' disposition, I guess. A year ago I was in Californy, but things didn't pan out very well, so when I read accounts of the goldfields out here, I jist dropped my pick and started, and here I am."

"Didn't you find any gold-dust in California?" asked Fletcher, with sudden interest.

"Well, I found *some*," answered the Yankee, with drawling deliberation, "but not enough to satisfy me. You see," he added, "I've got two to make money for."

"And who are those two?" inquired Fletcher.

"The first is my old dad—he's gettin' kinder broken down, and can't work as well as he could when he was a young man. He's got a thousand-dollar mortgage on his farm, and I want to pay that off. It'll kinder ease the old man's mind."

"That's a very excellent object, Mr. Stackpole," said Harry, who felt still more drawn to his plain, ungainly, but evidently good-hearted companion.

"I think so myself," said Obed simply.

"The other person is your wife, I fancy," said Fletcher.

"I expect she will be my wife when I get forehanded enough," replied Obed. "It's Suke Stanwood, one of Farmer Stanwood's gals. We was raised together, and we've been engaged for nigh on to five years."

"Very romantic!" said Fletcher, but there was a veiled sneer in his tone, as he scanned with contemptuous amusement the ungainly figure of his Yankee companion.

"I don't know much about such things," said Obed, "but I guess Suke and I will pull together well."

"You are not exactly a young man," said Fletcher. "You've waited some time."

"I'm thirty-nine last birthday," said Obed. "I was engaged ten years ago, but the girl didn't know her own mind, and she ran off with a man that came along with a photograph saloon. I guess it's just as well, for she was always rather flighty."

"It is very strange she should have deserted a man of your attractions," said Fletcher, with a smile.

Harry was indignant at this open ridicule of so honest and worthy a fellow as Stackpole, and he wondered whether the Yankee would be obtuse enough not to see it. His doubt was soon solved.

"It looks to me as if you was pokin' fun at me, Fletcher," said Obed, with a quiet, steady look at the other. "I'm a good-natured fellow in the main, but I don't stand any nonsense. I know very well I'm a rough-looking chap, and I don't mind your sayin' so, but I ain't willin' to be laughed at."

"My dear fellow," said Fletcher smoothly, "you quite mistake my meaning, I assure you. I am the last person to laugh at you. I think you are too modest, though. You are what may be called a 'rough diamond.'"

"I accept your apology, Fletcher," said Obed. "If no offence was meant, none is taken. I don't know much about diamonds, rough or smooth, but at any rate I ain't a paste one."

"A good hit! Bravo!" laughed Fletcher. "You are a man of great penetration, Stackpole, and a decided acquisition to our party."

"I'm glad you think so," said Obed dryly. "If I remember right, you didn't want me to join you."

"At first I did not, but I have changed my mind. I didn't know you then."

"And I don't know you *now*," said Obed bluntly. "If you don't mind, s'pose you tell us what brought you out here."

Fletcher frowned, and regarded the Yankee suspiciously, as if seeking his motive in asking this question, but his suspicions were dissipated by a glance at that honest face, and he answered lightly, "Really, there isn't much to tell. My father was a merchant of Manchester, and tried to make me follow in his steps, but I was inclined to be wild, incurred some debts, and finally threw up business and came out here."

"Have you prospered as far as you've gone?"

"Yes and no. I've made money and I've spent it, and the accounts are about even."

"That means you haven't much left."

"Right you are, my friend, but in your steady company I mean to turn over a new leaf, and go in for money and respectability. Now I've made a clean breast of it, and you know all about me."

In spite of this statement there was not one of his three companions who did not feel sure that there was much in Fletcher's history which he had kept concealed, and possibly for very good reasons.

The path of a gold-seeker in Australia was beset with difficulties. The country about Melbourne, and far inland, was boggy, the soil being volcanic, and abounding in mud which appears to have no bottom. The road to the mines was all the worse for having been ploughed up by bullock teams, and worked into a slough which proved the discouragement of mining parties. Some were even months in traversing the comparatively small distance across the country to the goal they sought. But the attraction of money, which is said to make the mare go, enabled them to triumph at last over the obstacles that intervened. It was not long before our party began to understand the nature of the task they had undertaken. The cart sank up to the hubs in a bog, and the oxen stood still in patient despair.

"Well, if this don't beat all creation!" ejaculated Obed. "I've been in the Western States, and I thought I knew something about mud, but Australy's ahead. I say, Fletcher, is there much of this that we've got to go through?"

"Mud's the rule, and dry land the exception," answered Fletcher coolly.

"Well, that's comfortin'!" remarked Stackpole, drawing a deep breath. "I s'pose people do get through after a while."

"Yes, generally. I was six weeks getting to the Ovens once."

"I wish we had some ovens to bake this mud," said Obed, with a grim smile at his joke. "It would take a powerful large one."

There was nothing for it but dogged perseverance. It took an hour to get the oxen and cart through a bog a hundred feet across, and the appearance of the party, when they finally reached the other side, was more picturesque than attractive.

Arrived on the other side of the bog, they were obliged to give the tired cattle a rest. Indeed, they needed rest themselves.

At the end of the day they made an encampment. As well as they could judge, they were about eight miles from Melbourne.

"Eight miles; and how far is the whole distance?" asked Harry.

"About a hundred miles," answered Fletcher.

"At this rate we can go through in twelve or thirteen days, then."

"You mustn't expect this rate of speed," said Fletcher. "We shan't average over five miles."

"Well, I hope we'll get paid for it," said Obed. "If we don't I'd better have stayed in Californy. We haven't any such mines as this in that country."

"You'd better have stayed there," said Fletcher dryly, and he evidently wished that his companion had done so.

The travellers encamped for the night in a dry spot among a group of gum trees, and it may readily be believed that all slept well. The boys felt dead tired, and it was with difficulty they were awakened in the morning.

About five o'clock Fletcher opened his eyes. He was one who slept fast, so to speak, and obtained as much refreshment from an hour's sleep as most people do from a period twice as long. He had been lying on the ground wrapped in a blanket, as was the case with the other members of the party.

Raising himself, and leaning on his elbow, he saw that they were all fast asleep. He nodded with satisfaction, and getting on his feet he approached Obed Stackpole with noiseless tread. The Yankee was sleeping with his mouth wide open, occasionally emitting a sonorous snore through his aquiline nose. He was not beautiful to look upon, as Fletcher evidently thought.

"Ill-favoured brute!" he ejaculated. "I'd like to choke him!"

If any special advantage had been likely to accrue to him, Fletcher's conscience would not have been likely to stand in the way of violence; but his purpose now was different.

"The fellow must have gold about him," muttered Fletcher. "I wonder whether I can get at it without waking him up."

Obed seemed to be in a profound slumber, but it was a peculiarity of our Yankee friend to wake at the least touch. This, of course, was not known to Dick Fletcher, who felt that there would be no risk in a careful exploration of Obed's pockets.

He thrust his hand into one of the Yankee's pockets with the practised skill of a pickpocket, when an entirely unexpected result followed.

"Why, you skunk, what in creation are you about?" exclaimed Obed, suddenly seizing Fletcher by the throat.

"Let me go!" said Fletcher, struggling violently, but ineffectually, to free himself.

"Not till you've told me what you are after."

"Let go, and I'll tell you."

Obed loosened his grip, saying sternly, "Are you a pickpocket, my enterprising friend, or what is the meaning of all this business?"

"You had better not insult me!" said Fletcher angrily. "I'm no more a pickpocket than you are."

"Then what is the meaning of your little game? Maybe you got up in your sleep."

"No, I didn't. I just waked up, and thought I'd like to have a smoke, but had no matches. I thought you might have some in your pocket."

"Why didn't you wake me up and ask me?"

"You looked so comfortable, and I thought you needed rest after a hard day's work, so I decided to help myself."

"It looks like it," responded Obed dryly. "So that's all you were after, was it?"

"Of course," said Fletcher, regaining confidence. "What else could it be?"

"Well, it strikes me it's rather takin' a liberty with a gentleman to search his pockets while he's asleep, that's all! In Californy, Fletcher, if you had been caught doin' it, ten chances to one you'd have been lynched, and lynchin' isn't usually regarded as comfortable or desirable. Where's your cigar?"

"I haven't any, but I've got a pipe."

"Well, I do happen to have a few matches in my other pocket, but I'd rather you'd ask for 'em next time."

"I will. The fact is, I ought to have brought some with me. It's very strange, old traveller as I am."

"It would have been a little better than borrowin' them of a sleepin' man without leave. Don't do it again, Fletcher."

CHAPTER IV
A VICTIM OF TREACHERY

"**I** MISTRUST that man Fletcher," said Obed to Harry Vane the next day, taking the opportunity when, at one of their rests, the man referred to had sauntered into the woods.

"I don't like him myself," said Harry. "Have you any particular reason for mistrusting him?"

"He was searchin' my pockets last night when he thought I was asleep," answered Obed, and he related the incident of the night before.

"It looks suspicious," said Harry. "I have not much money, but I don't care to lose what I have."

"I should like to shake him, but I don't see how we can very well. He's a reg'lar member of the party."

"We can be on our guard at any rate," said Harry. "I'll tell Jack, and advise him to be careful also."

At this point Dick Fletcher returned. He looked suspiciously from one to the other, under the impression that something had been said about him. He asked no questions, however, and no information was volunteered. He could not but observe, however, that there was more or less restraint in the manner of his companions toward him, and that they were not disposed to be social.

That day they made nine miles, the road being slightly better than the day before. About five o'clock they reached a rude wayside inn, over the door of which was a swinging sign, on which was printed:

TRAVELLERS' REST.

"We might as well stop here, instead of camping out," said Fletcher.

"I'm agreeable," said Obed, "if the tax isn't too high."

"Oh, Linton is moderate in his charges," said Fletcher. "I've known him a good while. He's a good fellow."

This was not a very valuable recommendation in the opinion of Obed and the two boys, but they had no objection to becoming guests of the establishment.

It was a rude building, and the accommodations were very limited. In fact, there were but two sleeping rooms. One of these Fletcher occupied, and the other was given up to the other members of the party, there being two beds.

"I'd rather bunk in with you, if you don't mind," said Stackpole to Harry. "I don't feel easy in the same room with Fletcher."

"We shall be very glad of your company, Mr. Stackpole."

"If I snore, just come and turn me over. I don't want to disturb nobody."

"I think Jack and I will be too sound asleep to be disturbed by your snoring," said Harry, with a laugh. "However, if there is any occasion, I will follow your directions."

The landlord was a broad-shouldered man of moderate stature, who had lost the sight of one eye. The other, being covered with a green shade, gave him an ill look. His manner, however, was hearty, and showed a bluff, offhand cordiality, as he welcomed the party to the hospitalities of the Travellers' Rest. He was familiarly called "Larry" by Fletcher, who greeted him like an old comrade.

The supper consisted in part of their own supplies, with some small additions from the larder of the inn. It was, at any rate, an improvement upon their camp fare, and the boys enjoyed it.

After supper they sat down on a settle in front of the inn, but presently Fletcher strayed away into the woods at the back of the house. Some fifteen minutes later Larry Linton also got up, but ostentatiously went in a different direction.

"I'm going a little ways to a squatter's to speak about some vegetables," he said.

"If you don't mind company, I'll go along too," said Obed.

"Better not," answered Larry. "There's a boggy spot which a stranger is likely to fall into."

"I've had enough of bogs," said Obed, shrugging his shoulders. "Seems to me you haven't got much besides bogs out in Australy."

So Linton went off by himself. After he was fairly out of the way, Obed said, turning to the two boys, "Did you think I wanted to go off with Linton?"

"I supposed so, as you made the proposal."

"I only wanted to find out if he wanted me or not. I have my suspicions."

"What kind of suspicions?"

Harry was the speaker, as usual, for Jack never took the lead when Harry was present.

"Fletcher and Linton are too thick together to suit me," answered the Yankee. "Looks as if they was in league together."

"Do you think they have arranged a meeting?"

"That's just what I do think."

"But they have gone in different directions," objected Jack.

"Bless your simple heart, my boy, that's done on purpose," said Obed. "Can't they fetch round together without our knowing it?"

"I didn't think of that," Jack admitted.

"Mr. Stackpole," said Harry, after a moment's thought, "if you and Jack will keep each other company, I will explore a little myself. I may happen to be at the conference."

"Be careful if you do, Harry," said Obed. "Don't run no risk."

"I'll look out for that."

In the rear of the house, and almost reaching to it, was a forest of eucalyptus trees. It was unfavourable to Harry's purpose that these trees rise straight from the ground, and are not encumbered with underbrush. It was very pleasant walking though, and Harry sauntered along at his leisure. He almost forgot the object of his enterprise, until some half-an-hour later, in the stillness of the woods, his quick ear caught the sound of voices.

He was instantly on the alert. The voices, he doubted not, were those of Dick Fletcher and Larry Linton. He moved forward cautiously, and soon espied the speakers. They were sitting on the ground, under the over-reaching boughs of a gigantic tree. Harry managed to get near enough to listen to the conversation, being himself concealed from view behind the trunk of a neighbouring tree.

"Is there much money in the party?" he heard Linton ask.

"I can't tell you. The boys haven't got much, but that long-legged Yankee has probably got considerable."

"What sort of a man is he?"

"He's likely to prove a troublesome customer. He is muscular, as you can see, and not easily scared."

"Has he any suspicion of you?"

"Yes; I put my foot in it the other night."

"How's that?"

"I saw him sleeping like a boy, and thought there was no danger of his waking up, so I took the liberty to explore his pockets. Before I could say Jack Robinson he had me by the throat, and wanted to know what I was after."

"That was awkward. How did you get out of it?"

"Lied out! Told him I was looking for matches, as I wanted a smoke."

"Did he swallow it down?"

"He didn't contradict me, but it has made him watchful and suspicious. If I'd got the money, I was ready to make tracks, and leave them to find their way as they could."

At this point the two rose and walked away, leaving Harry in his position behind the tree. As soon as he thought it was safe he came out, and made the best of his way to the inn, getting there about fifteen minutes before Fletcher appeared, but without the landlord. During that interval he had time to communicate what he had heard to Obed Stackpole.

"Just what I expected!" said Obed. "The treacherous skunk! So he's in league with the landlord, is he? I'll fix him."

He cautioned the two boys not to show by their manner that they had made any discovery, but to appear as usual.

The next morning the party started as usual. They plodded on for almost a mile, when Obed, turning quickly to Fletcher, said:

"Let me look at that weapon of yours a minute."

Fletcher unsuspiciously handed it over.

"I think I shall *keep* this, Fletcher," said Obed, eyeing him steadily. "I'm pained to have to bid you good-bye."

"What does all this mean?" blustered Fletcher.

"It means that your room is better than your company. We'd better part."

"Would you rob me? That revolver is mine, and I paid for a share of the things in the cart."

"I'll allow you the vally of them and pay you on the spot, but we can't go on together."

Suiting the action to the word, Mr. Stackpole handed over a handsome sum of money.

"But I don't want to sell my revolver," repeated Fletcher. "What am I to do out here alone and unarmed?"

"You'd better go back to your friend Larry Linton. He'll look out for you."

"You will regret this high-handed proceeding!" exclaimed Fletcher angrily.

"Maybe I shall, and maybe I shan't," answered Obed indifferently. "I'll risk it."

Fletcher halted a moment as if undecided, then turned back, and was soon out of sight.

All the party felt relieved to be rid of Fletcher. Without being able to prove anything against him, all believed him to be unworthy of confidence.

"I feel about tired out," said Obed, about the middle of the afternoon, just after he had extricated the team, by great personal effort, from a morass. "If I'd 'a' known as much of the country before startin' I wouldn't have started at all."

"It's a long road that has no ending," said Harry, smiling. He, too, was very tired, but youth is hopeful.

"It's the worst country I ever travelled in, by a long shot. If I ever make my pile I'll take the first steamer back to Frisco."

"Who's that?" suddenly exclaimed Jack.

Obed and Harry, looking up, saw a forlorn-looking figure approaching them. It was a man of middle age, and emaciated in appearance, looking the image of despair. He tottered rather than walked, from exceeding weakness.

"For Heaven's sake give me something to eat! I am almost famished," he cried.

"Why, certainly, friend," answered Obed, rising and advancing to meet the stranger. "We don't keep a first-class hotel, but you're welcome to what we've got. Are you travellin' alone?"

"Yes, if you call it travelling. I've been dragging myself along for several days, hoping to find somebody that would give me aid."

"Well, you've found somebody. Here, sit down, for you don't seem able to stand, and we'll provide for you. Harry, bring some biscuits and cold meat, won't you, and Jack had better build a fire. A cup of tea will put new life into you, my friend."

The biscuits were soaked in water and given to the stranger. He devoured them like a man in the last stages of hunger.

"Go slow, my friend. Your stomach must be weak," said Obed.

"If you only knew the gnawing at my vitals," said the newcomer. "I have not tasted food for three days."

"I never was in that fix, though I did go hungry for twenty-four hours once in Californy."

"That goes to the right spot," said the stranger, after he had gulped down two cups of tea. "Now I'm ready to die without complaining."

"If it's all the same to you, I think you'd better get ready to live," said Obed.

"I'd rather die now than suffer as I have done in the last three days."

"You won't have to. We've got plenty and to spare."

"But I have no money. I have been robbed of everything."

"Robbed! How is that?"

"It's rather a long story. You may not have patience to hear it."

"We've got time enough, and patience enough, but perhaps you don't feel strong enough to talk."

"I didn't before you relieved my hunger. The food and the tea have put new life into me, as you predicted they would."

"Then go ahead, stranger. We're all anxious to hear your story."

"I am an Englishman," began the unknown, "and my name is Ralph Granger. When the report reached England of the richness of the Australian goldfields, I sold out my business, and was among the first to come out here. By the sale of my business I realised about five hundred pounds. Three hundred I left with my wife—I have no children—to keep her while I was gone. It is very fortunate that I took this precaution and left her so well provided for, since had I brought all my money with me, it would all have been lost."

The three adventurers looked at each other soberly. The ill fortune of their new acquaintance did not augur very well for their good fortune.

"Then you had bad luck," said Harry inquiringly.

"On the contrary I had good luck," replied the stranger.

"Good luck!" repeated Harry in surprise. "Then how——"

"How did I come into this plight? That is what you were about to ask?"

"Yes."

"You will soon learn. On reaching this country I was in doubt whether to go to Ballarat or Bendigo but finally decided upon the latter."

"We are bound for Bendigo," said Jack.

"So I inferred. Ballarat is in a different direction. Very well, I reached Bendigo three months since. For a time I was unlucky. I found next to no gold, and the prices of living used up about all the money I had left after the expense of getting there. Just when I was on the point of giving up in despair I made a strike, and during the next six weeks I unearthed gold to the value of a thousand pounds."

"That certainly wasn't bad fortune."

"It was extraordinarily good fortune, and naturally drew the attention of the rest of the camp. This was unfortunate, for in such a settlement, as may well be supposed, there are many reckless adventurers, ex-convicts, and men utterly destitute of principle."

"Then you were robbed at the camp?"

"Not then nor there. I took the precaution to send the greater part of my money to Melbourne by experts. Destitute and lost, I have six hundred pounds in Melbourne awaiting my arrival; but for all that, I should probably have starved to death but for my opportune meeting with you."

"Come, then, you've got something to live for after all," said Obed.

"Yes, you are right. Let me once get to Melbourne and I am all right. I shall buy a passage ticket to Liverpool, and carry with me the balance of my money. With all that I have lost I shall go home richer than I came."

"But how did you lose your money?" asked Jack who was eager to have his curiosity gratified.

"When I got ready to leave the goldfields, there was no party which I could join. I did not like to go alone. In this emergency a man who had been working an adjoining claim offered to go with me. I saw no reason to distrust him, and accepted his proposal. All went pleasantly for three days, but on the morning of the fourth day when I awoke I found myself alone. A little startled, I felt for my gold, which I carried in a belt around my waist. It was gone, and so was my horse. Of course you guess how it happened. My companion had robbed me during the night, and left me in the woods utterly destitute."

"What was the name of your companion?" asked Obed quickly.

"He called himself Fletcher."

"I thought so!" exclaimed Obed, slapping his leg with emphasis. "We know the gentleman a little ourselves."

CHAPTER V
A DISAGREEABLE SURPRISE

"YOU have not met Dick Fletcher?" said Ralph Granger in surprise.

"Yes, we only parted from him this morning."

"Did he rob you?"

"No, but he tried to."

Here Obed gave an account of Fletcher's searching his pockets during the night.

"I am afraid he will turn up again," said Granger apprehensively.

"We'll try to be ready for him," said Obed coolly, "but I don't mean to borrow any trouble."

By this time their new acquaintance had satisfied his hunger. He turned gratefully to Obed Stackpole.

"How can I thank you for your great kindness?" he said earnestly. "I feel that you have saved my life."

"Tut, tut," said Obed, "I've only done as you would have done in my place. How long is it since you parted company with that skunk, Fletcher?"

"I think it is only seven days, but it has seemed a month."

"And didn't you meet anybody humane enough to relieve your hunger?"

"During the first four days, but not for the last three. Part of the time I lost my way, and did not meet any one. I hope you will never know such torments as I have known in that time."

"Amen to that! And now, my friend, what are your plans?"

"I should like to go back to Melbourne," said the stranger hesitatingly.

"If you say so, we'll fit you out with three days' provisions, and you can push on."

"I hardly like to go alone."

"I am sorry, for your sake, that we are going the other way. You see we haven't made our pile yet, and must go on. I'll tell you what you'd better do, Granger. Come along with us, and join the first party we meet bound for the city. You will, at all events, be sure of your victuals till then."

"I believe your advice to be good, and will accept your kind invitation. The tea and food have put new life in me, and my strength has returned."

They did not travel long together, however, for before nightfall they fell in with a party of eight persons bound for Melbourne, who agreed to let him join them.

"Good-bye, Granger," said Obed, as they parted. "I think you're all right now."

Toward the close of the day they entered a much pleasanter country. In place of sandy clay, baked hard in the sun, alternating here and there with a moist bog, they came to tall grass, trees of great height, and meadows suitable for grazing. The cattle revelled in the rich feed, and Obed suffered them to eat their fill, feeling that they had worked hard and deserved it. Though it was rather earlier than usual, they decided to encamp for the night near the margin of a creek, shaded by trees of a gigantic size.

They slept soundly all night, but they got ready to move at seven, the boys having made sure of a bath first. They were not to proceed far, however. About ten o'clock, as they were skirting the woods, six men on horseback rode out from the leafy covert. They seemed inclined to dispute the passage of the party.

"What can they want?" ejaculated Harry, with a startled look.
"I expect they are bushrangers," said Obed.

CHAPTER VI
FLETCHER TURNS UP AGAIN

ARRY didn't need to be told that bushrangers in Australia correspond to bandits in Italy and highwaymen in other countries. Stories of their outrages were common enough, and among the dangers apprehended in a journey to or from the mines, that of meeting with a party of this gentry was perhaps the most dreaded.

Though Obed Stackpole betrayed no emotion, but was outwardly quiet, his heart sank within him when he saw the bushrangers strung along the road.

Meanwhile Harry had been scanning the faces of the men who confronted them, and made a surprising discovery.

"Look, Obed," he said eagerly, "at that man on the extreme right."

Mr. Stackpole did look.

"Dick Fletcher!" he ejaculated.

But at this point the leader of the bushrangers broke silence.

"Do you surrender?" he asked in brief, commanding accents.

"I think we shall have to, squire," answered Obed, to whom the demand was naturally addressed.

"You must give up what money you have about you," was the next demand.

"It's mighty inconvenient, squire. I'm a good many thousand miles away from home, and——"

"Peace, fool! Produce whatever you have of value."

"I haven't got much. You've tackled the wrong man, squire."

"Fletcher, search that man!" said the captain of the band.

Dick Fletcher dismounted from his horse, and with evident alacrity advanced to the side of the Yankee.

"I think we've met before," said Obed significantly.

"I think we have," said the outlaw, showing his teeth. "I told you we should meet again."

"I can't say I'm overjoyed at the meeting. However, I respect you more now, when you show yourself in your true colours, than when you sneaked up to me at night, and searched my pockets, pretending all the while to be a friend."

"Take care how you talk!" said Fletcher, frowning. "Yesterday you were three to one, now you are in my power."

"So you're a highway robber, are you, Fletcher? Well, I can't say I'm very much surprised. I guess that's what you're most fit for."

"Do you want me to kill you?" said Fletcher, touching his hip pocket. "It isn't safe for you to insult me."

"Just so! You have a right to be brave with all them men at your side."

"What are you doing there, Dick Fletcher? Why don't you proceed to business?" demanded the leader impatiently.

"Empty your pockets, Stackpole!" said Fletcher, in a peremptory tone.

"All right."

The Yankee plunged his hands into his pockets, and produced in succession a jack-knife, a plug of tobacco, a bunch of keys, and a couple of buttons.

"Take them, Fletcher," he said, "if you want 'em more than I do."

"What do you mean with this tomfoolery?" demanded Fletcher, perceiving an impatient frown on the face of his chief. "Hand over your money."

"I guess you'll have to search me, Fletcher. You've done it before," answered Obed imperturbably. "I've mislaid my money, and you may know where it is better than I do."

Fletcher took him at his word, and proceeded to search, using some roughness about it.

"Be careful, Fletcher," said Obed. "I'm a tender plant, and mustn't be roughly handled."

Every pocket was searched, but no money was found. Dick Fletcher looked puzzled.

"I can't find anything," he said to the captain.

"Rip open his clothes," said the leader impatiently. "He has some place of concealment for his gold, but it won't avail. We shall find it."

Fletcher whipped out a knife and was about to obey directions, but Obed anticipated him.

"I'll save you the trouble, Fletcher," he said. "As you're bound to have the money, I may as well give it up. Just hand over that jack-knife, won't you?"

Fletcher hesitated, not understanding his meaning.

"Oh, I'll give it back to you if you want it, but I need it to get the money."

Upon this the knife was given back to him.

Obed cut open the lining of his pantaloons, and drew out four five-pound bank-notes. They were creased and soiled, but this did not impair their value.

"I guess that's what you were after," said Obed. "I can't say you're welcome to them, but that doesn't make any difference to you, I take it."

"Is that all you've got?" demanded the chief of the bushrangers, looking very much disappointed.

"Every cent, squire."

The leader turned to Fletcher.

"Didn't you tell us this man was well fixed?" he asked.

"I thought so," answered Fletcher, crestfallen.

"I thought you *knew* it. Why, this is a contemptibly small sum, and doesn't pay for our trouble."

"You're right, squire," said Obed. "It ain't worth carryin' away. You may as well give it back, Fletcher."

"That's a different matter," continued the captain. "Once more, is that all the money you have about you?"

"It is, squire."

"Be careful what you say, for if we catch you in a lie, we'll string you up to the nearest tree."

"It's as true as preachin', squire. I never lie. I'm like Washington. I dare say you've heard of him."

A further search was made, but no money was found, luckily for Obed, since there is reason to believe that the outlaw would have carried out his threat.

"The fellow here fooled you, Fletcher," said the captain sternly. "Take care how you bring us any more false reports."

"There are the boys," suggested Fletcher uncomfortable under the rebuke.

"Search them also."

This was done, or rather it would have been done, had not Harry and Jack, fully realising the futility of resistance, produced promptly all the money they had. So much, however, had been spent on the outfit, that between them they could only muster about seven pounds.

"Humph!" said the captain contemptuously, "that's a big haul, upon my word!"

"There are the cattle and supplies," said Fletcher.

"They will be of use. Here, Peter, do you and Hugh drive the team into the woods, and prepare some dinner for the band. We will be there directly."

Two men, unmounted, who seemed to be servants, came forward, and proceeded to obey orders.

"Hold on, squire!" exclaimed Obed in alarm "You ain't goin' to take our team, are you?"

"Most certainly I am. If you had had a large sum in money, we would have spared you this. As it is, we must have them."

"But we shall starve, without money or food."

"That is nothing to me."

"Well, boys, come along," said Obed in a despondent tone. "Our prospects ain't over bright, but something may turn up."

Meanwhile there was a quiet conference among the bushrangers.

"Hold!" said the captain, as Harry and Jack were about to leave the scene with their older companion. "*You* can go," turning to Obed, "but the boys remain with us."

Harry and Jack exchanged a glance of dismay. To be stripped of all they had was a serious misfortune, but in addition to be made prisoners by the bushrangers was something of which they had not dreamed. Obed, too, was taken aback. He had become attached to his young companions, and he was very sorry to part with them. He could not forbear a remonstrance.

"Look here, squire," he said familiarly to the captain, "what do you want to keep the boys for? They won't do you any good, and it'll cost considerable to keep 'em. They're pretty hearty."

Harry and Jack could not help laughing at this practical argument.

The captain of the bushrangers frowned.

"I am the best judge of that," he said. "You are lucky to be let off yourself. Don't meddle with matters that don't concern you."

"Take me, if you want to," said Obed independently. "I shall be lonesome without the boys."

"You had better go while there is a chance," said the captain menacingly. "If you give me any more trouble, I will have my men tie you to a tree and leave you here."

Harry was afraid the threat would be carried out, and begged Obed to make no further intercession.

"I have no doubt we shall meet again," he said. "These gentlemen will no doubt release us soon."

He was by no means confident of this, but he thought it politic to take things cheerfully.

"The boy has sense," said the captain approvingly.

"Well, good-bye, boys," said Obed, wringing the hands of his two young friends. "I shall feel awfully lonely, that's a fact, but as you say, we may meet again."

"Good-bye, Obed," said each boy, trying not to look as sorrowful as he felt.

Obed Stackpole turned and walked slowly away. His prospects were by no means bright, for he was left without money or provisions in the Australian wilderness, but at that moment he thought only of losing the companionship of the two boys, and was troubled by the thought that they might come to harm among the bushrangers.

"If I only knew where they were goin' to take 'em," he said to himself, "I'd foller and see if I couldn't help 'em to escape."

To follow at once, however, he felt would be in the highest degree imprudent, and he continued to move away slowly, but without any definite idea of where he intended to go.

"Follow me, men," said the leader. He turned his horse's head and rode into the wood.

The eucalyptus trees are very tall, some attaining a height of hundreds of feet. They begin to branch high up, and there being little if any underbrush in the neighbourhood, there was nothing to prevent the passage of mounted horsemen. The ground was dry also, and the absence of bogs and marshy ground was felt to be a great relief.

The boys were on foot, and so were two or three of the bushranger's party. As already intimated, they were of inferior rank and employed as attendants. In general the party was silent, and the boys overheard a little conversation between the captain and Dick Fletcher, who rode beside him.

"You haven't distinguished yourself this time, Fletcher," said the chief in a dissatisfied tone. "You led me to think that this party had money enough to repay us for our trouble."

"It isn't my fault," said Fletcher, in an apologetic tone. "The Yankee completely deceived me. He was always boasting of his money."

"He doesn't seem like that kind of a man," said the captain thoughtfully. "What could have been his object?"

"He must have meant to fool me. I am ashamed to say he did."

"Couldn't you have found out whether his boasts were correct?"

"That is just what I tried to do," answered Fletcher. "I crept to his side early one morning, and began to explore his pockets, but he woke up in an instant and cut up rough. He seized me by the throat, and I thought he would choke me. That made me think all the more that he carried a good deal of money about with him."

"The boys, too—did you think they were worth plundering?"

"Oh, no, I never was deceived about them," replied Fletcher promptly. "I concluded that, even if they had money, the Yankee was their guardian, and took care of it. They are all Americans, you know."

He spoke glibly, and the captain appeared to credit his statements. The boys listened with interest and with a new appreciation of Fletcher's character. They could easily have disproved one of his statements, for they knew very well that Obed never boasted of his money, nor gave any one a right to suppose that he carried much with him. On this point he was very reticent, and neither of them knew much of his circumstances. However, it would have done no good to contradict Fletcher, for his word with the captain would have outweighed theirs, and he would have found a way to punish them for their interference.

"In future," said the captain, "I advise you to make sure that the game is worth bagging. As it is, you have led us on a fool's errand."

"That may be," Fletcher admitted, "but it wasn't so last time. The Scotch merchant bled freely, you must allow."

"Yes, you did better then."

As Harry listened he began to understand that Fletcher acted as a decoy, to ingratiate himself with parties leaving Melbourne for the mines, and then giving secret information to the bushrangers with whom he was connected, enabling them to attack and plunder his unsuspecting companions.

"That's a pretty mean sort of business," he said to Jack, when he had an opportunity to speak to him without being overheard. "I'd rather be a robber right out than lure people into danger."

"So would I," responded Jack. "That Fletcher's worse than a pirate."

So they went on, but slowly, that the boys, though compelled to walk, had little difficulty in keeping up. They were necessarily anxious, but their predominant feeling was of curiosity as to their destination, and as to the bushrangers' mode of life.

At length they came out of the woods into more open ground.

On a slight rise stood a collection of huts, covered with sheets of the bark of the gum-tree, held on by ties of bullock hide. For the most part they contained but one room each. One, however, was large, and, the boys afterwards learned, was occupied by the captain of the bushrangers. Another served as a stable for the horses of the party.

This Harry judged to be the home of the outlaws, for no sooner had they come in sight of it than they leaped from their horses and led them up to the stable, relieving them of their saddles. Then the bushrangers sat down on the ground, and lounged at their ease. The attendants forthwith made preparations for a meal, appropriating the stores which had just been taken from Obed and the boys. The captives were not sorry that there was a prospect of a meal, for by this time they were hungry. They followed the example of their companions, and threw themselves down on the ground.

Next to them was a young bushranger, apparently about twenty-two years of age, who had a pleasant face, indicative of good humour.

"How do you like our home?" he asked, turning to Harry with a smile.

"It is a pleasant place," answered Harry.

"How would you like to live here?"

"I don't think I should like it," Harry replied honestly.

"And why not? Is it not better than to be pent up in a city? Here we breathe the pure air of the woods; we listen to the songs of the birds; we are not chained to the desk or confined from morning till night in a close office."

"That is true, but are there not some things you do not like about it," asked Harry significantly.

"Such as what?"

"Is it not better to earn your living, even if you are chained to a desk, than to get it as you do?"

Harry felt that he was rather bold in asking this question, but he was reassured by the pleasant face of the young outlaw.

"Well," admitted the latter, "there are some objections to our life."

"It would not do for all to get their living as you do."

"That is true. Some must work, in order that others may relieve them of a portion of their property."

"Are you not afraid of being interfered with?"

"By the mounted police?"

"Yes."

"We are strong enough to overcome them," said the bushranger carelessly.

"What is the name of your captain?" asked Harry.

"Stockton. No doubt you heard of him in Melbourne."

Harry shook his head.

The outlaw seemed surprised. "I thought everybody in Australia had heard of Ben Stockton," he said. "He has a great name," he added with evident pride. "He is as strong as a lion, fears nothing, and his name is associated with some of the most daring robberies that have ever taken place in this country."

"And still he is free," said Harry suggestively.

"The authorities are afraid of him. They have offered a reward for his capture, but it doesn't trouble him. He only laughs at it."

They were far enough away from the rest of the party to carry on their conversation unheard—otherwise, neither Harry nor his informant would have ventured to speak with so much freedom. At this eulogium, however, Harry scanned, with some curiosity, the face and figure of the famous bushranger, who was sitting about three rods distant. He was a man of large frame, powerfully built, with hair and beard black as night, and keen, penetrating eyes that seemed to look through those upon whom they were fixed. He had about him an air of command and conscious authority, so that the merest stranger could not mistake his office. About his mouth there was something which indicated sternness and cruelty. He was a man to inspire fear, and Harry, after a steady examination, felt no surprise at the man's reputation.

"How long has he been captain?" asked Harry.

"Ever since I joined the band," answered the young man. "I don't know how much longer."

"How long have you been a member of the band?"

"Five years."

"You must have been a mere boy when you joined."

"I was seventeen. I am twenty-two now."

"I should like to ask you a question, but you may not like to answer it."

"Go on! If I don't care to answer, I will tell you so."

"What induced you to join the bushrangers?"

"I will tell you," said the young man, showing neither offence nor reluctance. "I was employed in Melbourne in a business establishment. One of my fellow-clerks stole some money, and, to screen himself, managed to implicate me by concealing a part of the stolen money in my coat pocket. I knew no way to prove my innocence, and my employer was not a man to show pity, so I escaped from Melbourne and took refuge in the bush. There I fell in with Captain Stockton, who offered me a place in his band. I accepted, and here I am."

"But for the act of your fellow-clerk you would have been an honest business man to-day, then?"

"Very likely."

"What a pity!" said Harry regretfully, for he was much attracted by the open face and pleasant manners of the young man.

"So I thought at first, but I became used to it. After a while I grew to like the free life of the bush."

"I don't call it free. You can't go back to Melbourne for fear of arrest."

"Oh yes, I have been there several times," said the young man carelessly.

"How did you manage it?" asked Harry, puzzled.

"I disguised myself. Sometimes the captain sends me on special business."

"Like Fletcher?" asked Harry quickly.

"No; I shouldn't like that work. It suits him, however."

"I never should have taken you for a bushranger. You look too honest."

The other laughed.

"I think I was meant to be an honest man," he said. "That is, I am better suited to it. But fate ordained otherwise."

"Fate?"

"Yes; I believe that everything that happens to us is fated, and could not have been otherwise."

"You think, then, that you were fated to be a bushranger?"

"I am sure of it."

"That, then, accounts for it not troubling you."

"You are right. We can't kick against fate, you know."

"I shouldn't like to believe as you do," said Harry earnestly.

"You'll come to believe it sooner or later," said the outlaw, with an air of conviction.

"Then what is the use of trying to lead a good and honourable life?"

"That's just what I say. There isn't any use."

Harry had never before met any one holding such views of fate. He was interested but repelled. He felt that he could not and would not accept any such idea, and he said so.

"You'll change your mind after you become one of us," said his companion.

"After what?" ejaculated Harry.

"I suppose you know you are to become one of us."

"But that will never be. How can you think such a thing!"

"Because I know it is to be. Why do you think the captain brought you here? He had your money, and couldn't get any more out of you."

"Do you really mean what you say?" asked Harry, his heart filled with a sickening apprehension that this might be true.

"Of course I do. The captain likes young people. You two boys are smart and bright, and he is going to make you members of the band."

"He can't! I'll die first!" exclaimed Harry, with suppressed energy.

"You will see. But hush! don't speak so loud. For my part I shall be very glad to have you among us."

At this moment their companion was called away, and Harry, bending toward Jack, whispered in his ear: "I am afraid he is right about the captain's intentions. We must try to escape as soon as there is any chance."

"I'm with you," Jack whispered back.

CHAPTER VII
A TRIAL AND ITS TRAGIC FINALE

ARRY was very much disturbed by the communication of his new acquaintance, whose name he ascertained to be Wyman. It was not very pleasant, of course, to be a prisoner, but this he could have borne, being confident, sooner or later, of escaping. But to be forced to join these lawless men, and render himself, like them, an outlaw and outcast from respectable society, seemed terrible. He determined that, come what would, he would preserve his integrity and his honest name. He might be ill-treated, but they could not force him to become a bushranger. He talked the matter over with Jack, and the young sailor agreed with him.

Presently the meal was ready, and the two boys were served with the rest. Notwithstanding their precarious position, each ate heartily. It takes a good deal to spoil the appetite of a growing boy.

After eating, the captain, clearing his throat, addressed the band.

"My men," he said, "we have refreshed ourselves by eating, and now a less pleasant scene awaits us. I am your captain, and to me you have sworn implicit obedience. Is it not so?"

"Yes, yes!" answered the bushrangers.

"But one thing is essential. There must be no traitor, no malcontents among us. A large reward has been offered for my apprehension—five thousand pounds! It shows how much they are afraid of us," and he raised his head with conscious pride. "Against open enemies we can hold our own, but not against the secret foe who sits beside us as a friend, and eats and drinks with us. When such a one is found, what shall be his fate?"

He paused for a reply, and it came from the lips of all in one stern word—"Death!"

"I am answered," said the captain. "The sentence has been pronounced, not by my lips but by your own."

Here he turned to two attendants, who were stationed near at hand. "Bring forth the traitor," he said.

The two men disappeared within one of the huts, and immediately reappeared, leading behind them a third, with his hands tied behind him. His face was covered by a black cloth, which effectually screened his features.

"Complete your task!" said the captain, with a wave of his hand.

The two guards set the offender with his back to a tree, and producing a rope, quickly passed it round his waist and tied him securely, with his screened face toward the band.

"Wretch!" said the captain in a terrible voice, "you thought to betray us, and expose us to punishment and death, but the doom which you were ready to bring upon us has recoiled upon yourself. You would have sold your captain and comrades for gold. They have pronounced your doom, and it is *Death*! Have you anything to say?"

The victim did not speak, but slowly inclined his head in hopeless submission to his fate.

"You have nothing to say for yourself. Is there any one to speak for you?"

One of the bushrangers sprang forward impetuously. "Yes, captain, I will speak for him."

Captain Stockton frowned fiercely, but uttered one word, "Speak!"

The daring outlaw, who had stepped forward a little from the line, commenced: "This man is my brother. We were nursed by the same mother, we played together by the same fireside, we grew into manhood together, and together we joined this band of brothers."

He paused a moment, and the captain said briefly, "Well?"

"Now," continued the brother, "you would condemn him to a shameful death, which he does not deserve."

"Was he not caught attempting to escape? Answer me instantly."

"Yes, but he had no intention of betraying any of us."

"What then was his object?" demanded Captain Stockton sternly.

"He meant to leave you. He had become tired of the life of a bushranger. He wished to return to the paths of honesty, and live by labour at some respectable trade."

"And why was this? Why, after so many years, had he become tired of our noble independence?"

"In one of his missions, undertaken in the interest of the fraternity, he had made the acquaintance of a young girl, modest and attractive. He wished to marry her, but as a bushranger he knew this was impossible. Therefore, he resolved to leave our band, and enter upon a new life. He would never have uttered a word to imperil the safety of his captain or his comrades."

"And you expect us to believe this?" said the captain with a sneer.

"I do. I swear it is true."

"And what do you expect me to do, Robert Graham?"

"To consider his temptations, and to show mercy upon him."

"Perhaps also you expect me to release him, and bid him go his way to the maiden who is waiting for him."

"It would be a generous act."

"But I am not so generous," said the captain. "Your plea is ingenious, but I put no faith in it. It is utterly improbable. What he sought was blood money."

"No, a thousand times, no!" exclaimed the brother earnestly.

"I say it is so," said Captain Stockton harshly. "It is plain to every member of the band. Yet, because you have never transgressed I have been willing to listen to you, remembering that he is your brother."

"Spare his life at least; even if you are convinced that he is guilty. He has not lived his life half out. Be merciful!"

"I cannot," answered the captain, in an inflexible tone. "If I yielded to such a weakness all discipline would be at an end. If treachery is pardoned, who knows which one among you might be the next to imitate the example of this man. No! justice is stern, and punishment must be inflicted. The guilty must be punished though the heavens fall. Men, stand aside!"

This was addressed to the two men who stood, one on each side of the condemned bushranger.

They obeyed the command of their chief, and he, raising his revolver, pointed it at the breast of the unhappy offender.

There was a moment of intense excitement, Harry and Jack were spellbound.

The silence was broken by a sharp, explosive sound. The deadly weapon had done its work; but it was not the captive who had received the winged messenger of death. It was the captain himself who staggered, and with one convulsive movement fell prone to the earth.

The excitement among the bushrangers was intense. Simultaneously they started forward, and two of them, bending over, lifted the body of their prostrate leader. But he was already dead.

Robert Graham, the man who had caused his death, stood erect and unflinching.

He threw his weapon upon the ground, folded his arms, and said, in a tone devoid of fear: "Comrades, do with me what you will. I could not help doing what I did. It was either my brother's life or his. Sandy was innocent of the crime charged against him. Is there any one among you that would stand by and see his brother murdered before his eyes when he had the means of preventing it?"

The bushrangers looked at each other in doubt. They had at first accepted the captain's statement that Sandy Graham was a traitor. His brother's explanation of his attempted desertion put a new face on the matter. Then, again, there was not one among them that had not tired of their despotic leader. Alive, he had impressed them with fear, but he was far from popular, and had no real friend among them. It was a moment of doubt when a leader was wanted.

"Well," said Robert Graham, after a pause, "what are you going to do with me? I wait your pleasure."

"He ought to be served as he served the captain," said Fletcher, who disliked Graham.

"I say no," rejoined Rupert Ring, a man of medium height, but of great muscular development. "It was a terrible deed, but had my brother been in Sandy Graham's shoes, I would have done the same."

There was a half murmur, which seemed like approval.

"I move, therefore, that we pass over Robert Graham's deed as one to which he was impelled by brotherly affection, and that we restore Sandy Graham to his place in our ranks, on condition that he does not repeat the offence. Those who agree with me, hold up their right hands."

All hands were raised except that of Fletcher.

"Release the prisoner," said Ring, turning to the two attendants.

Instantly the rope was cut, the dark cloth was removed, and Sandy Graham, a tall, athletic, good-looking fellow, stepped forth, his face pale from the terrible strain to which he had been subjected.

"Comrades, brothers," he said, in a voice indicating deep emotion, "I thank you for giving me back my life. It shall be devoted to your service."

The first to press forward and grasp his hand convulsively was his brother, Robert Graham.

"Robert," said Sandy, "but for your brave act I should have been lying dead instead of him," and he pointed, with a shudder, to the dead captain.

Their conversation was interrupted by Rupert Ring.

"Comrades," he said, "the captain is dead. We can do nothing without a leader. We should appoint one at once."

Here Fletcher pushed forward.

"I am the oldest in service among you," he said. "I was the trusted friend of Captain Stockton. I submit that I have the best claim to be your leader."

But among bushrangers, as in other communities, the man who is the most anxious to secure office is very apt to be left in the lurch. Now, it happened that Fletcher was by no means a favourite in the band. He was sly and sneaking in his methods, currying favour with the captain, even at the expense of manliness and self-respect, and there were serious doubts as to his courage. If he had been wiser, he would not have made a boast of his standing with the late leader, for the men were heartily tired of his tyranny, and resolved to elect some one in his place who bore no similarity to him.

Rupert Ring smiled slightly as he heard Fletcher's modest claim.

"Comrades," he said, "you have heard Fletcher's appeal. It is true that he is the oldest in service among you. It is for you to consider whether that entitles him to the post of leader. Those of you who are in favour of Dick Fletcher as your leader will signify it by raising your right hands."

Fletcher's eye wandered anxiously around the circle. To his chagrin not a single hand was raised save his own. There was a cheer of derision which brought an angry flush to his cheek.

Then a clear voice was heard. It was that of the young man, Wyman, whose conversation with the two boys has already been recorded.

"I nominate Rupert Ring for our leader," he said.

There was a chorus of approval, which emboldened Wyman to add: "As he can't very well put the question on his own nomination, I will do so. Those of you who want Ring for your captain, please hold up your right hands."

All hands were raised except that of Fletcher.

"That settles it," said Wyman, who was unversed in parliamentary language. "I call for three cheers for Captain Ring!"

The woods echoed to the lusty cheers of the bushrangers. It was evident, from the general expression of satisfaction, that the choice was a popular one.

"Comrades," said the new captain modestly, "I did not look for this promotion, as you may have thought from my taking the lead just now, but I saw that it was necessary for somebody to act. I don't know whether you have made a wise choice or not, but I will do my best to make you think so. Since I am your captain, it is my duty first to see that proper honour is paid to the remains of your late captain. Prepare a coffin, and at daybreak we will commit him to the earth."

"I would like to suggest," said Fletcher, "that the two boys"—here he turned in the direction where Harry and Jack had been standing, and ejaculated in dismay, "I don't see them. What has become of them?"

"They have taken advantage of the excitement and confusion to run away, I fancy," said the new captain quietly.

This was quite true. Just after the fatal shot had been fired, and the attention of all had been taken up by the tragedy, Harry had whispered to Jack, "Now's our time to escape, Jack. Follow me!"

"I'm with you," responded Jack promptly, and no one noticed the two as they vanished among the trees.

"Shall I go after them, Captain Ring?" asked Fletcher in excitement. "I'll take another man, and scour the woods for them."

"It is not necessary," said Ring indifferently. "Let them go! They would only be in our way."

"But," protested Fletcher, "Captain Stockton meant to take them into the band. They are bright and smart boys, and would grow up into useful members."

"Heaven forbid!" said Ring earnestly. "Our lives are spoiled already, and we have no chance but to continue. Leave them to grow up innocent."

"This is strange talk for a captain of bushrangers," said Fletcher, disappointed.

"Remember that I am your captain," retorted Ring sharply, "and don't attempt to interfere with me! Go, I would be alone."

Fletcher slunk away, mortified and disappointed. It was well for the two boys that he had not been elected captain.

CHAPTER VIII
LOST IN THE WOODS

ES, the boys had escaped. When the excitement produced by the fatal shot was at its height, it had flashed upon Harry like an inspiration that then, if ever, was the time to escape. He knew that it would be at the risk of their lives, and but for one consideration it is doubtful if he would have been willing to incur the peril of the attempt. But he felt that to stay was to run a risk as great—that of being compelled to join the ranks of the bushrangers, and of that he had a great dread.

They never stopped running till they had set half a mile between them and the camp of the bushrangers. Jack was the first to show distress.

"Hold on, Harry," he said, panting, "I'm all out of breath."

Harry instantly slackened his speed.

"Look back, Jack," he said anxiously; "and see if you can discover any one pursuing us."

"I see no one," answered Jack, after a prolonged look.

"They have other things to think of," said Harry. "The murder of their captain has put all thoughts of us out of their heads. When the excitement has subsided a little, I am afraid they will look for us. How terrible it was!" he added with a shudder.

"Yes," returned Jack. "I saw that man—the captive's brother—lift his weapon and point it at the captain. Almost before I could speak it was discharged and the captain fell. He must have been killed instantly."

"I little thought what lay before me when I left home," said Harry.

"I wish I knew what lies before us now," said Jack.

"I am afraid our prospects are rather dark. We must take care at any rate not to fall again into the hands of the bushrangers. I am most afraid of that man Fletcher. If he could have his way, he would show us no mercy."

"Let us go on again," said Jack. "I only stopped to catch my breath."

"You are right, Jack. The farther we get away from the bushrangers the better."

Before them was a densely wooded hill. The way had become difficult with the scrub bushes that filled up the distance between the trees.

"We can't make our way here, Harry," said Jack despondently.

"Oh yes, we can. Besides, don't you see, the rougher and more difficult the way, the less are we likely to be followed. I am willing to go through a good deal to escape capture."

"So am I," answered Jack. "You are always right. Push ahead, and I'll follow."

For three or four hours the boys kept on their way. They surmounted the hill, and found a clearer country. By this time it was growing dark, and the boys were feeling both fatigued and hungry.

"I think we can rest now, Jack," said Harry.

With a sigh of relief Jack threw himself on the ground.

"This is worse than any work I did on shipboard," he said.

Harry smiled.

"I don't think it is likely to cure you of your love for the sea, Jack," he said. "Though I haven't your fondness for sea life, I confess I would rather be on the deck of a good staunch ship than here."

"Harry," said Jack anxiously, "when do you think we shall find something to eat? I am terribly hungry."

"So am I, Jack. It's the hard walk that has increased our appetite."

"I have often thought I might be afloat in an open boat without anything to eat, but I never expected to be caught in such a pickle on land."

"A good many things have happened to us to-day that we didn't expect," said Harry. "Do you know, Jack, it seems the longest day I ever spent!"

"I can say the same."

"This morning we set out with Obed, free from care. We have been captured by bushrangers, taken to their camp, seen the murder of their leader, escaped, and after walking for miles through a rough wilderness here we are, tired out and in danger of starvation."

"Don't say any more, Harry," said Jack faintly. "I can realise it without your description."

"I wish Obed were with us," said Harry, after a pause. "Perhaps he could think of some way out of our trouble. He is an experienced man, and is used to roughing it. As for me, I feel helpless."

"Do you think there is likely to be any house near at hand?"

"It doesn't look like it," said Harry, shaking his head.

"I don't think I should mind much being caught and carried back by the bushrangers, if they would give me a good supper," said Jack ruefully.

"Poor Jack!" said Harry compassionately; "I do believe you are suffering for food."

"I told you so, Harry."

"My appetite no doubt will come later. At present I am not very uncomfortable. Well, Jack, there is only one thing to do. We must explore farther and see if we can find any trace of a human habitation. Suppose you go to yonder knoll, and climb the tree at the top. Then use your eyes for all they are worth."

Jack followed his advice, and with a sailor's agility mounted the tree. Then, shading his eyes with his hand, he looked earnestly, first in one direction, then in another.

"Well, Jack?" inquired Harry anxiously.

There was a pause; then Jack called out joyfully: "I see a light: yes, I am sure I see a light."

"Whereaway?"

"Straight ahead, or a little to the left."

"Take a good look, Jack, so as to be sure of your bearings. Then we will make our way toward it with the best speed we can muster."

Jack scrambled down from the tree with his face actually cheerful. The prospect of a meal had put new life into him.

"Follow me!" he said. "I don't think it can be more than a mile away."

Not feeling their fatigue so much now that they were buoyed up by the hope of shelter and food, the two boys plodded on. The way was at times difficult, and there was no glimpse of the light which Jack had seen from the tree-top.

"Do you think you are on the right track, Jack?" asked Harry anxiously.

"Yes, I feel sure of it," answered the young sailor.

Events proved that Jack was right. They came to an open place, from which they could distinctly see the light gleaming from a dwelling.

"There, what did I tell you?" demanded Jack triumphantly.

"You are right, Jack. I am glad enough to admit it. Now the question is, will the people who occupy the house let us in?"

"They can't be so inhuman as to refuse. Pass on, Harry."

They were not long in reaching the hut. It was one of those slab huts which are used by shepherds. They are lonely enough, the stations being in some instances twenty miles from the nearest dwelling. This was a single dwelling, the home of one of the outkeepers. The chief stations are usually an aggregation of dwellings. In the yard was a pile of wood for fuel. Close at hand was a paddock surrounded by a rail fence, over which hung a number of sheepskins. All these evidences of habitation cheered the hearts of the lonely boys.

Harry went up to the door and knocked.

His knock appeared to create some commotion inside. A voice was heard, and then there was audible the barking of a dog, but no one came to the door.

"Suppose you knock again, Harry," said Jack.

"They must have heard my first knock. Perhaps they don't want to let us in."

However, Harry knocked again.

Again the dog inside barked, this time with fierce emphasis.

"Is there no one inside but the dog?" thought Harry anxiously. Having no weapon with him, he took a piece of a broken rail, so that in case of necessity he might have a means of defence.

He was about to venture on a third knock when a tremulous voice, which the boys at once recognised as that of a girl, was heard from within.

"Who are you? What do you want?"

"We are two boys who have lost our way, and are almost starved," answered Harry. "For heaven's sake let us in, and give us something to eat."

There was a pause, the girl being evidently undecided.

"Are there only two of you?" she asked.

"Only two."

"You are sure there is no one with you?"

"No one."

"And you are boys?"

"Yes."

"What brings you here—in this lonely place, at this hour?"

"We are on our way to the goldfields of Bendigo."

"But this is off the road."

"I know it. The fact is, we were captured by the bushrangers, and have made our escape. We plunged into the woods, thinking we were less likely to be caught and carried back."

There was a change in the girl's tone as she said "Is this really true? Are you not bushrangers yourselves?"

"No, I hope not," answered Harry, with a boyish laugh.

This laugh, which sounded natural and genuine, evidently inspired the girl with confidence.

"If I let you in, will you promise to do no mischief?" she asked.

"You shall have no cause to regret admitting us, we promise that."

There was still a little pause of indecision, and then a bolt was drawn, and the door opened. The two boys saw in the doorway a pleasant-faced girl of fourteen, whose eyes fell upon them not without a shade of anxiety. But when she saw that the two visitors were boys not much older than herself, there was a look of relief, and she said, "I will trust you. Come in if you like. Hush, Bruno!"

This was addressed to a large shepherd dog that stood beside her, eyeing them suspiciously.

A weight seemed lifted from the hearts of the two boys as they caught sight of the comfortable interior of the hut. On the one side of the room was a large open fireplace, on which a good fire was burning. The flickering flames helped illumine the apartment, and diffused a home-like air, which was most grateful to the two tired wanderers.

"You are very kind to admit us," said Harry. "You have no idea how great a favour it is."

"I would have let you in before, but I thought you might be bushrangers," said the girl.

"We don't look much like bushrangers, do we?" said Harry, with a smile.

The girl smiled too. She was evidently pleased with the appearance of her two visitors.

"No; if I had seen you I should have known better than to think you belonged to their band. Come in and sit down by the fire."

"Thank you."

Harry and Jack seated themselves on a settle near the fire, and the girl continued to eye them curiously.

"I suppose you are boys," she said.

"We don't call ourselves men yet," answered Harry.

"I never saw a boy before," was the unexpected remark of their young hostess.

"WHAT!" ejaculated the two boys in concert.

"I scarcely ever saw anybody," explained the girl. "My father and I live here alone, and have lived here for years. He has a flock of fifteen hundred sheep to watch and tend. Sometimes another shepherd calls here, and we had a visit from the bushrangers last year."

"It must be very lonely for you," said Harry, in a sympathetic tone.

"Yes, it is; but I am used to it. Father is away all day, but he leaves Bruno to keep me company."

"Come here, Bruno!" said Jack, in a coaxing tone.

Bruno eyed Jack dubiously, and finally walked up to him deliberately, and allowed himself to be stroked.

"Bruno doesn't think we are bushrangers," said Jack, smiling.

"He did at first though," the girl replied, with an answering smile. "Have you been walking all day?"

"Yes, the greater part of the day."

"Then you must be hungry."

"We are almost starved!" said Harry tragically. "Are we not, Jack?"

"I am quite starved," said the young sailor.

"Then I must get you some supper," said the girl, in a hospitable tone.

"Thank you," said Harry earnestly. "Will you let me know your name?" he asked.

"My name is Lucy."

"My grandmother's name was Lucy," said Jack.

"Then you may look upon me as your grandmother," said the girl demurely.

Of course all three laughed heartily at this absurdity. Then Lucy moved about with quick steps, and soon a goodly supper of mutton-chops was fizzling in the frying-pan, sending forth savoury odours that made their mouths water. Presently Lucy drew out a table, and placed upon it the chops and some bread.

"I would boil some potatoes," she said, "but you might not like to wait so long."

"I think we won't wait, Lucy."

"You haven't told me your name," said Lucy, as they drew up to the table.

"My name is Harry Vane," said the possessor of that name.

"And mine is Jack Pendleton."

"Harry and Jack," repeated Lucy, nodding.

At this point Bruno raised his head, looked toward the door, and began to bark.

"I think my father must be close by," said Lucy. "Bruno is always the first to hear him."

Before Lucy could reach the door it was opened, and a stalwart man of middle age paused on the threshold in evident surprise.

"Whom have you here, Lucy?" he asked, in a tone of displeasure.

"Two boys, papa, who came here in distress, having lost their way."

"Did I not caution you against admitting strangers?" continued her father, with a slight frown.

"Yes, but these are boys, not men."

Harry Vane thought it was time to start.

"I hope, sir," he said, "you won't blame your daughter for her kindness to us. We stood greatly in need of friendly help, having been robbed of everything by the bushrangers, from whom we managed to escape some hours since."

The shepherd regarded Harry keenly, and proceeded to cross-examine him.

"You say you were captured by the bushrangers," he said.

"Yes, sir."

"When was this?"

"This morning, just after breakfast."

"Where did it happen?"

Harry told him.

"Where were you going?"

"To the mines at Bendigo."

"How large was your party?"

"There were only three of us—a countryman of ours and ourselves."

"Where is he?"

"The bushrangers robbed him and let him go."

"Why did they not release you and your friend?"

"Because, as a young member of the band told us, the captain meant to spare us to join the band."

"You are young to be travelling to the mines. Humph! your story sounds well enough, but how do I know that you are not spies of the bushrangers?"

Harry Vane's eyes flashed indignantly.

"I hope you won't think so badly of us," he said.

The shepherd seemed somewhat impressed by his indignant denial, which certainly seemed genuine enough, but wanted information on one point.

"How did you manage to escape? That doesn't seem very probable, at any rate."

"We both took advantage of the excitement occasioned by the murder of Captain Stockton——" he began.

"What!" exclaimed the shepherd, in profound astonishment. "Captain Stockton murdered! When? By whom?"

Of course Harry told the story, but that need not be repeated.

The shepherd listened in evident excitement.

"If this is true," he said, "nothing better could have happened for this part of Australia. This man—Stockton—is noted everywhere as the most desperate and cruel of the bushrangers. I can't begin to tell you how many atrocious crimes he has committed. He killed my brother in cold blood three years since"—here the shepherd's face darkened—"because he defended the property of another, and tried to save it from being stolen. If he is dead I am deeply, profoundly grateful!"

"You need have no doubt on that point, sir," said Harry. "Jack and myself saw him shot down. There can be no doubt of his death."

"I believe you speak the truth. You don't look as if you were deceiving me. So you took the opportunity to give the bushrangers legbail, eh?"

"We didn't stay to bid them good-bye," said Harry, smiling. "We ran till we were out of breath, but saw no one on our track. Probably it was some time before we were thought of and our escape noticed. We have been walking ever since, and were ready to drop with hunger and fatigue when we espied your cottage, and ventured to ask for help."

"You are welcome to all that we can do for you," said the shepherd, his tone changing. "I was suspicious at first, for the bushrangers are up to all sorts of tricks, but the news you have brought insures you a welcome. At last my poor brother is avenged, and the bloodthirsty villain who killed him has gone to his account. You don't know who is elected in his place?"

"No, sir, we came away at once."

"Of course, of course; I should have thought of that."

"I hope it isn't Fletcher," said Jack.

"Ha! what do you know of Dick Fletcher?"

"More than we want to. He it was who passed himself off on us as a returned miner, and betrayed us into the hands of his comrades."

"I know of him, too. He would be as bad as the captain if he dared, but he is a coward. His turn will come after a while. But, Lucy"—here he addressed his daughter—"you are not treating your guests very well. Where are your potatoes and other vegetables?"

"They were so hungry they preferred not to wait for them, papa."

"You may put them in the pot now. I want them, and I think our young friends will be able to eat them later."

"You are very kind, sir, but I am afraid Jack and I will not be able to compensate you. The bushrangers took all we had, and left us penniless."

"I don't want your money, boy. You are welcome to all you get in this house. We don't have visitors very often. When they do come, they have no bills to pay."

"Unless they are bushrangers, father!" said Lucy, with a smile.

"If they are bushrangers they will meet with a still warmer reception. And now, daughter," said the shepherd, "hurry up supper, for I have a very fair appetite myself."

Lucy moved about quietly but actively in obedience to her father's directions. An hour later, or perhaps less, the table was spread once more, and all got up to it. The boys, though the edge of their appetite was taken away, managed to eat the vegetables with a relish, not having had a chance to eat any for a considerable time.

After supper they sat down beside the fire and talked. Living so much alone, the shepherd and his daughter were anxious to hear all that the boys could tell them of the great world from which they lived aloof. Later in the evening, the shepherd, whose name, by the way, was Andrew Campbell, said, "Now, let us have a little music. Lucy, bring me the bagpipe."

His daughter went into an adjoining room, and brought out a Highland bagpipe, which Campbell received, and straightway began to play upon it some characteristic Scotch tunes. It was loud and harsh, but the boys enjoyed it for want of better.

"Don't you sing, Miss Lucy?" asked Harry, when her father laid down the instrument.

"No," answered the girl, smiling. "I wish I did. Father is very fond of singing."

"Aye, am I; Lucy's mother sang, but the gift has not descended to her."

"Harry is a professional singer," said Jack. "He sings in public."

"Please sing something, then," pleaded Lucy.

"If you really wish it," answered Harry.

"I shall be glad to hear you, young sir," said the shepherd.

Harry hesitated no longer, but sang at once, choosing such Scotch melodies as he knew in preference. The shepherd's eyes glistened, and he was evidently much moved.

"It calls back my early days, when as a lad I trod the heath in Scotland," he said. "You are a fine singer. I don't mind when I have enjoyed an evening as much."

"I am very glad, sir, if I have been able in this way to repay your kindness," said Harry.

"Don't speak of it, lad," said the shepherd, lapsing into his Scotch mode of speech. "We shan't miss the bit sup we have given you."

At nine o'clock all retired for the night, for the shepherd must be up early in the morning to look after his flocks. Harry and Jack slept in a small room at the back. They were very tired, and fell asleep as soon as their heads struck the pillow.

CHAPTER IX
A DANGEROUS ACQUAINTANCE

THOUGH the boys were very much fatigued, they were up in time for an early breakfast the next morning. It consisted of mutton-chops, potatoes, bread, and coffee, and they were prepared, notwithstanding their hearty supper of the night before, to do full justice to it.

The shepherd had got over his first impression, and nothing could be more friendly than his manner toward them. He gave a still stronger proof of his confidence and friendship.

"So you think of going to the mines, my lads," he said.

"Yes, sir."

"I don't know about the wisdom of your plans. It isn't all that find the gold they look for. Are you expecting to come back with fortunes?"

"They would not be unwelcome, sir," said Harry, "but we shall at any rate like the advantage of it, and we are young enough to try experiments."

"That's true; but about the gold I'm thinkin' you'll be disappointed. At any rate I'll make you an offer—the two of you. Stay here and help me tend sheep. I'll give you your living and clothes, and when you are twenty-one, I will make you a present of a hundred sheep each to start in business for yourselves."

The proposal took Harry and Jack by surprise. They could not but observe that Lucy's face brightened with hope as she awaited their answer. It was clear that she hoped it would be favourable. It must be acknowledged that this made a considerable impression upon them. Lucy was a pretty girl, and they felt flattered by her desire that they should remain. But their resolution was only shaken, not changed. They had but to look about them at the unbroken solitude to feel that life under such circumstances would be unendurable. Both of them had led lives of activity and excitement, and neither felt prepared to settle down, but they felt grateful.

"Jack and I thank you for your kindness, Mr. Campbell," said Harry, "and consider your offer a good one. But it would be lonely for us here, and, though we may change our minds, we would like to try the goldfields first."

"It's only natural, lads," said the shepherd. "You are young, and you crave excitement. When you are as old as I am, you won't mind the quiet. But if you have bad luck at Bendigo come back here, and you shall be welcome to stay as long as you like, and to accept my offer if you feel like it then."

"I am sorry you won't stay," said Lucy, with a shade of sadness.

"I wish we could be contented to do so," said Harry. "You may be sure we won't forget your kindness, Miss Campbell."

"Do you mean me?" asked Lucy, smiling. "I never was called Miss Campbell before."

"I will say Lucy, if you will allow me."

"I would rather you did."

"Then good-bye, Lucy. We shall always remember you."

"And you will come back some day?"

"If we can."

"Then good-bye, and don't forget your promise."

There was a suspicious moisture in the girl's eyes, for she knew that when the young visitors were gone she would feel lonelier than ever.

"That's a nice girl, Jack," said Harry, after a pause.

"That's so, Harry. I never saw a girl so nice before," responded Jack emphatically.

"Do you know, Jack," said Harry, turning to him with a smile, "it is just as well we are going away."

"What do you mean, Harry?"

"If we stayed here till we were both young men, we might both fall in love with Lucy, and quarrel over her."

"I might fall in love with her, but I would never quarrel with you, Harry," said Jack affectionately.

"No, Jack, I don't think you would. Nothing shall ever divide us."

"You are very kind to a poor sailor boy," said Jack. "You know a great deal more than I, and I am not fit to be your friend."

"Take care, Jack, I may quarrel with you if you say anything against yourself. Fit or unfit, you are my chosen friend, and I should not be willing to exchange you for any one else I have ever met."

The boys did not set out on their journey empty handed. Lucy, by direction of her father, had packed a basket with provisions enough to last them two or three days. The shepherd wished also to lend them some money, but this Harry declined.

"We might not be able to pay it back," he said.

"I shan't miss it, lads, if you don't," urged the shepherd.

"We might be robbed of it as we were of our other money, sir. We thank you all the same."

But they gladly accepted the basket of provisions, without which, indeed, they might have fared badly in that uninhabited wilderness.

"How far is it to Bendigo?" Harry had asked the shepherd.

"Twenty miles or thereabouts," was the answer. "You will be fortunate, however, if you reach there in three or four days."

"If it were a straight road and good travelling we might be there by night. Give us the direction, and we will try it, sir."

The two young travellers, refreshed by their night's sleep and two substantial meals, made good progress, and by noon found themselves, despite the difficulties of the way, seven miles distant from the station where they had received such hospitable treatment. By this time they were hungry, and were glad to sit down at the base of a gigantic gum-tree and attack the provisions they had brought with them. They were in good spirits and chatted cheerfully. Many thousands of miles away from home, without a penny in their pockets, and with only a basket of provisions between them and starvation, they did not allow themselves to be depressed by their uncertain prospects, but looked forward hopefully.

"Jack," said Harry, "it seems so lonely here, I could easily believe that we two are alone in the world."

"It does seem so," said Jack.

"I feel a little like Robinson Crusoe on his island."

"Am I to be Friday?" asked Jack, with a smile.

Jack had read very few books, but who is there who has not read Robinson Crusoe?

"I don't think you are of the right colour, Jack, but I would a good deal rather have you than Friday."

They were not so far away from human companionship as they supposed, as they soon learned to their dismay. Suddenly they heard a crunching as of steps upon the brush, and turning, they saw, with alarm, a tall muscular man, with matted locks unprotected by a hat, a long untrimmed beard, and a suit hanging in tatters over his gaunt, bony figure. His eyes were fixed with a famished look upon the open basket of provisions.

The boys started to their feet in affright.

"Give me food!" said the stranger, in a hoarse voice.

Harry took some bread and meat from the basket and handed them to the stranger, who devoured them in silence. His appetite seemed enormous, and the boys saw in dismay that if he kept on there would be very little left. It was necessary in self-defence to limit the man's rapacity.

"More, more!" he cried, when he had eaten all that had been given him.

"We have given you all we can spare," said Harry firmly.

"Give me the basket, or I will kill you both!" exclaimed the tramp, his eyes suffused with blood, and gleaming with fierce anger.

As he spoke he raised a knotted stick which had served him as a cane, and swung it menacingly above his head.

Harry and Jack were brave boys, and not easily daunted, but the attitude of the stranger was so menacing, and his frame so indicative of strength, that they were both alarmed. Had their need of the provisions been less urgent they would have surrendered them without a struggle, but they felt that it was a question possibly of continued life or starvation, and this inspired them to resistance.

Holding the basket in his hand, Harry retreated behind a tree, and began to parley.

"You are asking too much," he said. "We have given you a meal. We need the rest for ourselves."

"No palavering, boy!" said the tramp roughly. "I need it more than you do. Give it to me, or I will kill you."

"If I only had some weapon," thought Harry.

While he was hesitating, the tramp, with a quick movement, sprang to where he stood, clutched him by the collar, and flinging him on his back put his knee on his breast, saying between his closed teeth, "Now I will kill you, young jackanapes! I'll teach you to interfere with me."

Poor Harry thought his last moment had come. He was powerless against his enemy, whose wild rage, shown in his distorted features, seemed capable of anything. His sole helper was Jack, who flung himself on the giant, and sought with his boyish strength to pull him away, but in vain.

"I'll choke the life out of you, you young beast!" exclaimed the tramp, preparing to clutch Harry by the throat. The moment was a critical one for the poor boy, whose career came near ending then and there.

But assistance came when least expected.

A man who had approached, unseen by either of the three, jumped from the underbrush, and with one powerful blow sent the tramp sprawling on the ground beside his intended victim.

"You're rather out of your reckoning, you mean skunk!" he exclaimed. "If there's any killin' to be done round here, I'm goin' to do it."

"Obed Stackpole!" ejaculated the boys in heart-felt delight, and they were rushing forward to greet him, but he waved them back.

"Yes," he said, "it's Obed himself. I'll talk to you in a minute, after I've got through with this consarned villain."

By this time the tramp, though startled and dazed, was on his feet, and preparing to make a desperate assault on the Yankee. But though quite as strong, and possibly stronger than Obed Stackpole, he had now to encounter a foe by no means to be despised. Moreover, he had laid down his knotted stick, and Obed had secured it. It was a formidable weapon, and Mr. Stackpole was quite ready to make use of it.

"Give me my stick!" shouted the tramp hoarsely.

"I mean to," responded the Yankee coolly. "Where will you have it?"

He stepped back warily, as the other advanced, holding the stick in a strong grasp, while he kept his eyes steadily fixed on his opponent. He was cool, but his enemy was enraged, and rage made him incautious.

He made a desperate clutch at the stick, but with a powerful sweep Obed struck him on the side of the head, and he fell like an ox, stunned and insensible.

"That settles you, my friend, I guess," said Obed. "You brought it upon yourself, and you've got no one else to blame. Watch him, Harry, to see that he doesn't come to himself, while I tie his hands."

Obed whipped a strong cord from his pockets, and secured the wrists of the prostrate enemy, tying them securely together.

"Will you tie his feet, too?" asked Jack.

"No, it is not necessary. He can't do any harm now. I came in the nick of time, boys, didn't I?"

"Indeed you did!" said Harry earnestly. "He was beginning to choke me."

"What was it all about?"

"We had given him a meal, but he wanted to make off with the basket besides. As this would have left us utterly without food, I objected."

"The mean skunk! I'm glad I came up in time to settle him."

"Won't you have something to eat yourself, Mr. Stackpole?" asked Harry, bethinking himself that his deliverer might need refreshment.

"I don't mind if I do," answered Obed. "The fact is, I'm feeling kinder hollow. I feel a gnawin' at my vitals that isn't pleasant. This is prime fodder; where did you raise it?"

While Obed was eating—with hearty relish, it may be added—Harry related briefly what had befallen Jack and himself since they had parted company.

"You're in luck, boys," was Obed's comment. "You fared better than I, for you've had your square meals, while I've had only one besides this."

"Where was that?" asked Harry.

"At the same place where you passed the night. I got there about an hour after you left, as well as I can make out. The gal was very kind, and gave me a tip-top breakfast. I ate till I was ashamed, and then left off hungry. That's why I've got such an appetite now. Yesterday I didn't have but one meal, and I've had to make up for that."

"Did Lucy tell you we had passed the night at her father's house?"

"Lucy! Seems to me you got mighty familiar," said Obed, in a jocular tone. "She didn't tell me what her name was. I suppose she looked upon me as a dried-up old bach."

"She's a nice girl," said Harry emphatically.

"So she is. I'm with you there. But about your question—I asked her if she had seen anything of two chaps about your size, and she told me enough to show me I was on your track. She told me which way you went, and I follered. She was a little shy at first, not knowin' but I might be an enemy of yours, but when she'd made up her mind to the *contrary* she up and told me everything. Well, I struck your trail, and here I am."

"I for one am delighted to see you, Obed," said Harry cordially.

"And I for two," added Jack, smiling.

Mr. Stackpole seemed gratified by the pleasure evinced by the boys.

"Well," he said, "we're together once more, and now we must hold a council of war, and decide what's to be done."

"With him?" asked Jack, pointing to the tramp.

"With him first of all; I take it you don't want me to invite him to join our party?"

"His room is better than his company," said Harry.

"I agree with you. According to my idea, we may as well leave him where he lies."

"But won't he starve?"

"He can get his hands free after awhile," said Obed, "but not till after we are at a safe distance. You needn't be afraid about him. Anyhow the world wouldn't lose much if he did take passage for another."

"That's so, Obed, but I wouldn't like to feel that we were responsible for his death."

At this moment the prostrate man opened his eyes, and as his glance lighted on Obed, they gleamed with the old look of rage. He tried to get up, and of course discovered that his hands were tied.

"Loosen my hands, you scoundrel!" he exclaimed.

"If you mean me by that pet name, my esteemed friend," said Obed, "I respectfully decline. I'd rather look at you with your hands tied."

"Do you want me to kill you?" demanded the tramp furiously.

"Not at present! when I do I'll let you know. Come, boys, we may as well be going. This gentleman would rather be left alone."

"Unloose me first, and I won't harm you," said the other, trying to struggle to his feet.

"I don't mean you shall. Good-bye, my friend. I can't say I wish to meet you again. I will take the liberty to carry off your stick, as you won't need it with your hands tied."

Obed and the boys started off, followed by the most fearful execrations from their late acquaintance. They had scarcely gone a quarter of a mile when they met two mounted police, who halted their horses and inquired: "Have you seen anything of a man, tall and spare, dark hair and eyes. We have traced him to this neighbourhood, and think he must be near."

"What has he done?" asked Obed curiously.

"Murdered a man at the mines in a drunken brawl."

"We've just parted company with him," said Obed. "I found him experimentin' on my young friend here, but come up in time to block his game."

"Put us on his track, and we will share the reward of a hundred pounds with you."

"I'll do it. Boys, stay here and I'll go back with these gentlemen. I'll join you in an hour."

Obed was as good as his word. Within an hour he was back again, with the two policemen, followed by the man whom we have called the tramp.

His hands were more securely fastened now by a pair of handcuffs.

CHAPTER X
THE BOYS ARRIVE AT BENDIGO

"OU are entitled to half the reward offered for the apprehension of this man," said the leader of the police to Obed Stackpole. "I congratulate you. Fifty pounds is a sum not to be despised."

"Especially when a man has been robbed of all he possesses by bushrangers," said Obed. "If you'll excuse me, captain, why does your government allow them rascals to roam round the country, plundering and killing honest men?"

The captain of police shrugged his shoulders.

"We can't help it, my good man. We do all we can," he answered.

"In my country we would soon put a stop to it."

"You mean America?"

"Yes; the land of the Stars and the Stripes," said Obed proudly.

"It is more difficult here," observed the police captain. "The nature of the country makes pursuit difficult. Besides, we have had so many convicts sent out here in past years that there is a large proportion of lawless men in the colony. Some of these men have made themselves very formidable. There is Captain Stockton, for instance."

"*Was*, you mean, captain."

"I don't understand you."

"Captain Stockton is dead."

"Do you mean this? How do you know?" inquired the captain of police eagerly.

"He was killed yesterday by one of his men."

"What evidence have you of this?" demanded the captain incredulously.

"Them two boys saw him shot," said Obed, indicating Harry and Jack.

"Tell me all about it, young man," said the captain to Harry. "It will be good news at Bendigo. Returning miners are always in fear of this famous bushranger, Stockton. He doesn't care so much to attack parties bound to the mines, for they are not supposed to have much with them, but those returning to Melbourne generally carry more or less gold, and are worth capturing."

Harry gave a succinct account of his adventures while in the power of the bushrangers, and the scene of which he had been a witness. The captain of police listened attentively.

"This is good news," he remarked. "There will be a new captain appointed, of course, but there is not another man connected with the gang who can take Stockton's place or do as much mischief as he has done."

"How far are we from Bendigo, captain?" asked Obed.

"Two days' journey, or perhaps more."

"A long distance, considering we have no money."

"You will have half the reward. Your share will be fifty pounds."

"That won't do us any good now, unless you'll be kind enough to advance us a part of that sum."

"I would if I were able, but I am not provided with any money beyond what I need. You and the boys may come with us, however, if you wish."

"I should like nothing better, captain. Once at Bendigo, and we'll manage to shift for ourselves."

"Very well, so let it be."

I pass over the events of the next two days. Obed and the boys, after all their troubles, found themselves provided with an official escort, and on the morning of the third day arrived at the famous goldfields of Bendigo.

Ballarat and Mount Alexander preceded Bendigo in point of time, but Bendigo has been far more productive. As the little party descended a hill made white by the sandy dirt thrown out of the mines, they saw below them Bendigo Creek, yellow as the Tiber, running sluggishly through the valley, which on either side had been dug up by prospectors for gold. All about on the slopes of the hills and in the valley were rude huts, hastily put together, the homes of the miners. Some of them were built of solid trunks of trees laid horizontally, after the backwoods order of architecture. The interstices were generally daubed with clay to make them water-tight, and the roofs were covered with sheets of bark, kept down by logs laid upon them. There were tents also, made of slabs, and covered with canvas. Still others were covered with bullock hides.

To Harry and Jack the sight was a novel one, and they regarded the extemporised village with interest.

Obed's eyes glistened, and he rubbed his hands with delight.

"This seems like home," he said. "It's just like Shantytown in Californy, where I worked three months last year. I say, boys, how do you like it?"

"I shouldn't like to live here very long," said Harry.

"I like shipboard better," said Jack.

"I agree with you, boys," said Obed, "but it'll suit me well enough if I can find enough gold here. When I've made my pile, Australy won't hold me long. I shall make tracks for home."

"But you have Indians," retorted the police captain, who did not quite relish the strictures upon the colony of which he was an official. "I would rather be captured by a bushranger than scalped by an Indian."

"I agree with you, captain, but the Indians won't scalp you unless you go where they are. I never saw one till I was past twenty-one."

"Indeed!" said the captain, in evident surprise. "I thought they were all over the country. Why, one of your countrymen told me they would sometimes surprise families within ten miles of your great city of New York, and scalp them all. He said he was brought up—raised, he called it—twenty miles away, and was obliged to barricade the doors and windows every night, and keep a supply of loaded muskets by the side of his bed, to resist the Indians in case they made a night attack."

Obed laughed till the tears came to his eyes, and the two boys also looked amused.

"Did you believe all this, captain?" he asked.

"Why not?" asked the captain, looking offended. "My informant was a countryman of yours."

"He was stuffing you, captain."

"*Stuffing* me! I don't understand," said the captain, puzzled.

"He saw that you knew very little of America, and he practised a little on your credulity—isn't that the word?"

"How do I know but you are doing the same now? Probably you want to give me a favourable idea of your country."

"I only want you to judge it correctly, captain. Why, there ain't no more danger of being scalped in New York than in London."

"I presume not, *in* New York, but I am speaking of the neighbourhood of New York."

"So am I. I'll tell you what, captain, if you can find me a case of a man that's been scalped within five hundred miles of New York within the last fifty years, I'll give you my share of the reward. Of course if it's in Canada, it don't count."

"I can't accept any such wager. I have no means of proving it, even if it is so."

By this time they had descended the hill, and were on the borders of the mining settlement. They had now attracted the attention of the miners, and when the prisoner was recognised there went up an angry shout, and a band of swarthy, bearded men advanced menacingly to meet them.

"Give him to us!" they cried. "Give up the murderer! We will make short work of him!"

The face of the prisoner, as he met the angry glances of the miners, betrayed extreme fear. In spite of his terrible crime, Harry could not help pitying him when he saw the grey pallor that overspread his countenance.

The captain of the police was a brave and determined man, and, though his little force was outnumbered five to one, he showed no signs of yielding.

"What is it you want, men?" he demanded sternly.

"We want that man—the murderer," was the unanimous cry.

"What would you do with him?"

"String him up to the nearest tree," replied a brawny miner.

"There is no occasion for you to punish him—he is in the hands of the law," replied the captain.

"He may escape. We want to make sure of him."

"I will answer for it that he does not escape. You know me, and you can accept my assurance. Is that satisfactory?"

There was a sullen murmur among the miners. It was evident that they were not wholly satisfied.

The captain of police watched them keenly, and saw that there was danger of an attack.

He drew a pistol, and holding it firmly in his hand, said: "The first man that interferes with me in the discharge of my duty, dies. I give you fair warning."

A determined man generally carries his point, even against odds. Had the captain showed the slightest sign of wavering, the mob would have been upon him. But they saw that he was in earnest, and meant what he said.

"How long is he to live?" asked the brawny miner already referred to, after a slight pause.

"I shall take him before the magistrate at once, and you know he is not likely to defer punishment."

The police magistrate who dispensed justice, and frequently injustice, at Bendigo, was noted for his severity, and this assurance seemed to satisfy the miners. They followed the cavalcade, however, to make sure that the captain kept his word. It may be stated here that, at this early period in the history of the colony, the judicial forms which prevail in other countries were for the most part dispensed with, and punishment was swift and certain, especially where life or property had been attacked.

Harry and Jack followed the crowd to a wooden structure more pretentious than most of the buildings roundabout. The magistrate—whom I will call Judge Wood—was at hand. He was a short, stout man of severe aspect, and had a harsh voice.

"Whom have we here?" he asked quickly.

The captain of police answered the question, relating also where and under what circumstances the capture was made.

"What have you to say for yourself, my man?" he asked, turning to the prisoner.

"I am innocent," was the reply, in trembling accents.

"Of course. You all are. I never had a man brought before me who was not innocent," said the magistrate, with a sneer. "Have you any accomplices?"

"Your honour, I am innocent, as I have already told you."

"Answer my question!" said the magistrate sternly.

"No, your honour."

"Ha! You alone are guilty then. Captain, are there any witnesses? though it is hardly necessary. The man's face shows his guilt."

It will easily be seen how much hope the prisoner had of getting off with such a judge presiding at the trial. Luckily for the cause of justice the man was undoubtedly guilty, and so the judicial proceedings, hurried and one-sided as they were, did not entail any injustice. In a short time the trial was ended, and the man convicted and sentenced to execution on the following morning. Meanwhile he was to be confined in a structure set apart as a prison.

"Well, are you satisfied?" asked the captain, as he passed the ringleader of the miners.

"I don't see the use of waiting till morning," grumbled the miner. "The job might as well have been finished up at once."

"You can rest satisfied. The man hasn't long to live."

This proved to be the case. During the night Harry and Jack, who were accommodated with beds in a hut near the prison, heard a noise and a sound of men's voices, but they were too fatigued and worn-out to be thoroughly roused. In the morning, when they left the hut, they needed no explanation. From a lofty branch of a gum-tree a hundred yards to the west dangled the body of the unfortunate criminal, a terrible spectacle, contrasting painfully with the bright and cheerful morning. They learned afterward that the prison had been guarded by a volunteer company of miners, who detected the prisoner in an attempt to escape, and forcing an entrance, laid violent hands upon him, and saved the law officers the trouble of executing him.

The captain of police didn't learn what had happened till morning. As it chanced, Obed Stackpole was with him when he received the information.

He took it very coolly.

"What are you goin' to do about it, captain?" asked Obed.

"Nothing."

"Do you allow such doin's here?"

"It doesn't matter much. The man was to have been executed this morning at any rate. He only lost a few hours. It has saved us some trouble."

"Suppose he was an innocent man?"

"But he wasn't, you know. And now, Mr. Stackpole, if you will come with me, I will see about your getting your share of the reward."

"Thank you, captain. I won't deny that it'll be particularly convenient, seein' I'm reduced to my last penny."

The police captain exerted himself in a very friendly manner, and owing to the absence of red tape which in an older settlement might have occasioned delay, that same day our Yankee friend was made happy by receiving the sum of fifty pounds.

He called the boys to him, and dividing the money, as well as he could, into three equal parts, he offered one each to Harry and Jack.

"Now we start alike," he said. "There's nearly seventeen pounds apiece. It seems a good deal, but it won't last long. We must find something to do before long."

"That's just what I want," said Harry; "I came out here to work, and make money, not to loaf about."

"That's the way with me," said Jack, but his tone was not so hopeful or cheerful as Harry's.

"Confess now, Jack," said Harry, "you would rather be on board ship than here at the diggings."

"I would," said Jack; "wouldn't you?"

"Not yet. There is no money to be made on board ship."

"When you've made your pile, my lad," said Obed, "you can go back to Melbourne, and easily get a berth on board some merchant ship bound to Liverpool or New York. There is a great demand for sailors at that port."

This made Jack more cheerful. He was willing to stay a while, he said, and help Harry and Mr. Stackpole, but in the end he must return to his old life.

Mr. Stackpole and the boys took a long walk, and reconnoitred the diggings on both sides of Bendigo creek. Towards the middle of the afternoon they came upon a thin, melancholy looking young man, who was sitting in a despondent attitude with his arms folded.

"Are you sick, my friend?" asked Obed.

"I am very ill," was the answer. "I don't think I shall ever be any better."

Further questioning elicited the information that he had taken a severe cold from exposure two months before, in consequence of which his lungs were seriously affected.

"Why do you stay here, then?" asked Obed.

"I shall go back to Melbourne as soon as I have sold my claim."

"What do you want for it?"

"It is worth fifty pounds. I will take twenty-five."

Obed after careful inquiry judged that it was a bargain. He proposed to the two boys to join him in the purchase of the claim. They felt that they could safely follow his judgment, and struck a bargain. So before twenty-four hours had passed, the three friends were joint proprietors of a claim, and had about eight pounds apiece to meet expenses till it began to yield a return.

CHAPTER XI
STRIKING LUCK

"OW, boys," said Obed, "we have some hard work before us. Mining isn't like standing behind a counter, or measuring off calico. It takes considerable more muscle."

"I am used to hard work," said Jack, "but you'll have to show me how."

"I'll keep up with Jack," said Harry manfully.

"You won't have to charge either of us with laziness."

"I believe you, boys. There isn't a lazy bone in either of you. As I have experience, I'll boss the job, and you'll have to obey orders."

"All right, captain!" said Jack, touching his cap, with a smile.

This, then, was the understanding between the three, and it was faithfully adhered to. The two boys, sensible of their ignorance, were very ready to obey Obed, and he found them willing workers. They installed themselves in a cabin which had been occupied by the man they bought out. He gave them the use of it, having no further occasion for it himself, and they began to keep house as one family. They lived roughly enough, and yet, so high were all articles of food, on account of the trouble and expense of transportation from Melbourne, that it cost them as much as would have paid for living at a respectable hotel at home.

All three entered upon their labours with high hopes. The first day and the second day yielded no results, but, as Obed reminded them, a miner needs to be patient. But when one week—two weeks—passed, and the amount of gold found amounted to less than two pounds, all three began to look sober.

"This is beginning to look serious, boys," said Obed thoughtfully, as they set about their work on the first day of the third week. "Our claim ain't pannin' out very rich."

"My store of money is panning out very fast," said Harry, with a faint smile.

"I've got less than two pounds left," said Jack. "What are we going to do when it's all gone?"

"I don't know," said Obed, "unless we catch another murderer."

The boys smiled, but not hilariously. They felt, as Obed expressed it, that matters were indeed becoming serious. To run short of money nearly ten thousand miles from home was no light thing.

"We might sell the claim," suggested Harry.

Obed shook his head.

"I don't think we could," he replied. "Everybody would understand our reason for selling—that we despaired of finding any gold—and instead of getting twenty-five pounds, I doubt if you could get twenty-five shillings for it. You know about how long twenty-five shillings would last us."

"I suppose there is nothing to do but to keep on," said Harry.

Obed nodded. "You've said it," he returned. "Let us keep up good heart, my boys. Don't borrow trouble. When things come to the worst we'll decide what to do then."

By way of setting the example of cheerfulness Obed began to whistle "Yankee Doodle," and the boys joined in. It was not altogether a successful effort, but it made them feel a little more cheerful. At all events it attracted a listener—a tall, shabby-looking tramp, who had been wandering about for a day or two, visiting one claim after another, trying to raise a loan.

"I say, you're uncommon jolly, you chaps," he began, as he stood in a lounging attitude watching the little party at their work.

"If we are it's a credit to us," returned Obed dryly, "for there isn't much to be jolly about."

"Isn't your claim a good one?"

"That's what we're trying to find out. Where's yours, stranger?"

The tramp returned an evasive answer and shambled off.

"Do you think he's got a claim, Obed?" asked Jack.

"No; but he's prowling around to see what he can pick up."

"Do you think he's a thief?"

"I think he's willing to be. He heard us whistling, and thought we'd found something."

"We are safe from robbery—for the present," said Harry.

"Yes, there's that advantage about being poor. It reminds me of old Jack Pierce in our village."

"What about him?" asked Harry.

"He read in the paper one day that a certain bank had burst. So he went home in a hurry to see if he had any bills on that bank. He found that he had no bills on that bank—or any other—and then he felt better."

Harry laughed.

"It was a poor consolation, I think," he said. "I remember hearing a sermon from our minister at home in which he said that riches were a great responsibility, but I don't think I should mind taking the responsibility."

"That's my idea, Harry. I am afraid there isn't much chance of our having that responsibility, but there's one thing we can do if we don't make the claim pay."

"What's that, Obed?"

"We can join the bushrangers."

"Will you set us the example?" asked Harry, smiling.

"I'm not quite desperate enough yet. We'll try the claim a little longer. But I'm gettin' tuckered out. We'll go and get some dinner, and then start diggin' again."

They repaired to their cabin, and solaced themselves with food. Then they threw themselves down in the shadow of the cabin to rest, and Obed pulled out his pipe. This was a solace which the boys didn't enjoy. They were sensible enough to know that, whatever may be said of men, boys only receive injury from the use of tobacco. In the resolution to abstain they were upheld and encouraged by Obed, who, veteran smoker as he was, did not approve of smoking.

"You're better off without it, boys," he said. "It won't do you no good. I wish I could leave it off."

"Why don't you?" asked Harry.

"Easier said than done, my boy. Let me see, I was only turned of thirteen when I used to slink off to the barn and smoke, for I knew father wouldn't let me if he knew it. It made me sick at first, but I thought it was makin' a man of me, and I kept on. Well, the habit's on me now, and it's hard to break. It don't hurt a man as much as a boy, but it don't do him any good either. Jack, did you ever smoke?"

"No, Obed; but one of the sailors gave me a piece of tobacco to chew once. I didn't like it and spat it out."

"The best thing you could do. I wish all boys were as sensible."

In their hours of rest the three often chatted of home. Their conversation was generally of one tenor. They liked to fancy themselves returning with plenty of money, and planned how they would act under such pleasant circumstances. Instead of the barren hills among which they were encamped, familiar scenes and faces rose before them, and the picture was so attractive that it was hard to come back to the cheerless reality.

"Well, boys," said Obed, at the end of an hour, "we may as well go to work again. The gold's waitin' for us."

It was an old joke, and scarcely elicited a smile now. In fact, the boys felt that they had waited a long time for the gold. It was not, therefore, with a very hopeful feeling that they obeyed the summons and returned to the claim. Though of a sanguine disposition, they began to doubt seriously whether their efforts would ever be rewarded. They had pretty much lost the stimulus of hope.

About four o'clock, when Jack was at work with the pick, something curious happened. Instead of sinking into the earth, it glanced off as from something hard.

"What is it, Jack?" asked Obed quickly.

"I must have struck a rock, Obed."

"Here, give me the pick," said Obed eagerly.

He struck, and lo! a yellow streak became plainly visible.

"Boys," said he, in an agitated voice, "I believe our luck has come."

"What do you mean, Obed?"

"I believe we've found a nugget;" and to the boys' intense surprise he immediately began to cover it up with dirt.

"What's that for?" asked Harry.

"Hush! we mustn't take it out now. Somebody might be looking. We'll wait till it's darker."

Just then a tramp strolled up.

"What luck, friends?" he asked.

"Same as usual," answered Obed, shrugging his shoulders. "Don't you want to buy the claim?"

"Not I,"—and the tramp, quite deceived by his manner, kept on his round.

"It's lucky we covered up the gold," said Obed, in a low voice. "That's the last man I wanted to discover our good luck."

"Shan't we keep on working?" asked Harry, in excitement.

"I will just probe a little to form some idea of the size of the nugget," answered Obed.

"Then you think it is a nugget?" asked Jack eagerly.

"Yes, I think our luck has come at last, boys. I think we will be able to pull stakes and go back home. But about keeping on now, we shall need to be cautious. Some one might come by, and see what we are about."

Then Harry made a suggestion.

"Let Jack go up to the top, and if any one comes he can whistle. That will put us on our guard."

"A good idea!" said Obed.

So Jack threw himself on the ground in a listless posture, and the other two continued their explorations. They dug all about the boulder, which proved to be about a foot in diameter. It was embedded in clay, from which it was separated with some difficulty. It was encased in quartz, but the interior was bright, glittering gold.

"It's a regular beauty," said Obed, in a low tone, his eyes glittering with excitement.

"How much do you think it's worth, Obed?" asked Harry, in the same low tone.

"That's hard tellin', Harry; but it's worth a thousand pounds easy."

"Thank God!" ejaculated Harry fervently. "That will release us from our imprisonment, and enable us to go back home."

"You are right, Harry, but the hardest job lies before us."

"What's that?"

"To get it out without observation, and keep it secure from thieves."

"We'll do our best. Only you give the orders, Obed."

"Then, first and foremost, we'll cover it up again, and go up till evening, when we will secure it and carry it to our cabin."

So said, so done. They joined Jack at the limit of the excavation.

"Is it all right?" asked the young sailor eagerly.

"Yes," answered Harry.

Jack was told of their plan of removing the nugget by night, and saw at once that it was a wise one.

"Shall we go to the cabin now?" he asked.

"No, Jack; it won't do to leave our treasure unguarded. We will lounge here, and make sure that no one robs us of our discovery."

So they sat down, and Obed lighted his pipe once more.

A neighbour strolled up and sat down beside them.

"You are leaving off work early," he said.

"Yes," answered Obed, with a yawn, "we might as well take it easy. It's hard work—this mining."

"What luck?"

"Our luck is to come," said our Yankee friend. "How is it with you?"

"I've got out seventy-five dollars this week," answered the other complacently.

"Whew! that's good! What do you say to swapping claims?"

"Oh no," answered the neighbour, wagging his head jocosely. "I'm not so green. The fact is, Mr. Stackpole, I don't want to discourage you, but I don't believe you'll ever see the money you put into this hole. Come now, what did you pay?"

"Five and twenty pounds."

"If you can get five pounds for it, my advice is sell."

"I don't know but you're right," said Stackpole in a rueful tone. "Will you give me five pounds for it?"

"Ho, ho! I might give you five shillings, though it would be a risk."

"Then I don't think we'll sell, eh, Harry?"

"We had better give it away than take that sum," said Harry, carefully veiling his inward exultation.

They went to their cabin at the usual time and indulged themselves in a better supper than usual, feeling that they could afford to do so. It is wonderful how success stimulates the appetite.

"I don't know when I have been so hungry, Obed," said Harry.

"I feel the same way," chimed in Jack.

"A light heart increases the appetite, boys, but sometimes I've felt wolfish when my heart was heavy. Fifteen months ago I was in Californy and down on my luck. Things had been goin' contrary, and I hadn't money enough to buy a square meal. I didn't like to tell my friends, bein' a bit proud. One day when I was feelin' so hungry that I wouldn't have turned up my nose at a Chinaman's diet—rat pie—an old acquaintance met me and asked me to dine with him. Did I accept? Well, I should smile. I did smile all over my face, as I sat down to the table. You'd better calculate that I made my knife and fork fly. Finally my friend remarked, looking kind of queer, 'You've got a healthy appetite, Stackpole.' I answered, 'It sort of runs in our family to eat whenever we get a chance.' 'Good joke!' said he, laughing. But it was no joke when he came to pay the bill, I tell you."

"I'll remember that, Obed," said Harry, smiling, "and when I invite you to dinner, I'll first inquire whether you've had anything to eat for a week back."

"I generally eat for a weak stomach," returned Obed, venturing on a little joke at which the boys felt bound to laugh.

As they sat at the door of their cabin, they kept a good lookout in the direction of their claim. They could not afford, now that success was in their grasp, to have it snatched away. But they discovered no suspicious movements on the part of any one. In fact, no one suspected that they had "struck it rich." So poor was the general opinion of their claim, that they would have found it hard to obtain a purchaser at any price. Had there been the least suspicion, the camp would have been greatly excited.

As a rule, the miners retired early. They became fatigued during the day, and sleep was welcome. There was, indeed, a gambling saloon at some distance, frequented by the more reckless, but generally good hours were observed in the camp.

About half-past eleven, Obed nudged Harry and Jack, who had fallen asleep.

"What is it?" asked Harry, in a drowsy tone.

"Hush!" whispered Obed. "Don't make any more noise than you can help. I think it will be safe to go and secure the nugget now."

This was enough. Harry was wide awake in an instant, and he in turn roused Jack.

There was no elaborate toilet to make, for they had thrown themselves down in their day attire. They left the cabin, and by the faint light of the moon, which was just ready to retire for the night, they found their way to the claim without being observed.

Fifteen minutes' work and the task was accomplished. The nugget was raised, and wrapped in a red bandanna handkerchief, which Obed had brought all the way from his New England home.

"It must weigh seventy-five pounds," whispered Obed exultantly. "Boys, we're in tall luck. It was worth coming out to Australy for. We'll keep it in the cabin over night, and to-morrow we'll put it where it will be safe."

They gained the cabin without having been seen so far as they knew. Of the hundreds of men sleeping within a furlong's distance, not one dreamed of a discovery which was to draw the attention of the whole colony to Bendigo. But they had not wholly escaped observation. One pair of eyes had detected them in their midnight walk.

CHAPTER XII
THE NUGGET IN DANGER

HE tramp, who has already been introduced to the reader, had spent the evening at the gambling house, having come into possession during the day of a small sum of money, given him by a compassionate miner. He had risked it, and for a time been successful, so that at the end of an hour he might have left off with twenty pounds. But the fatal fascination of the game drew him on till all his winnings melted away, and he left the cabin at midnight without a penny in his pocket, so far as he knew. There was, however, a shilling which he had overlooked, and did not discover till he was already some distance away. He was tempted to return, and probably would have done so, had not his roving eyes discovered Obed and the two boys returning from their claim with the nugget.

"What are they up to," he asked himself in amazement, "that keeps them out of bed till after midnight? There's something up. I wonder what it is."

He had reason to be surprised. With the exception of those who, like himself, spent the night in gambling (when he was in funds), no one in the camp was awake or stirring. And of all, none kept more regular hours than Obed and the two boys.

Casting about for some explanation, the tramp's attention was drawn to the burden that Obed carried.

"What can it be?" he asked himself wonderingly. Then, with a flash of conviction, he said to himself: "A nugget. They've found a nugget as sure as I'm a sinner."

The tramp was intensely excited. His covetous soul was stirred to its depths. The opportunity he had been waiting for so long had come at length. It meant fortune for him. Qualms of conscience about appropriating the property of another troubled him not at all. He meant to have the nugget, by fair means or foul.

The would-be thief understood well, however, that there would be difficulties in the way of accomplishing his design. Obed and the two boys were broad awake, and half-an-hour—perhaps an hour, must elapse before he could feel sure that they would be asleep. In the meantime it would be best to keep away from the cabin, lest some one inside might see him lurking near, and suspect his purpose.

While he is keeping watch from a distance, let us enter the cabin.

Obed and the boys are sitting on their rude pallets, congratulating themselves on having secured the nugget, and removed it from the mine unobserved. Harry had made a remark to that effect, when Obed Stackpole responded, "Do you know, boys, I feel sort of uneasy to-night."

"Why?" asked Jack.

"I'm afraid some one might have seen us on our way from the mine."

"I couldn't see anybody," Harry remarked.

"Nor I, but there may have been some one, nevertheless. The fact is, I never expected to be uneasy on account of my wealth, but that's the way the case stands just at present. When we were poor I slept like a top."

"I suppose you wouldn't care to get rid of your care by throwing the nugget away," Harry said, with a smile.

"I'm not so uneasy as that yet, but I should feel a little safer if we and the nugget could be transported to Melbourne in five minutes."

"Suppose some one did see us?" queried Jack.

"Then we may expect a visit some time to-night."

"One of us might remain awake, Obed."

"That would be rather hard on us, for we are all tired. I don't believe I could stay awake all night if I tried."

"Is there any way of concealing the nugget?"

"I don't know. If we had a cellar that would be a good place, but——"

"Stop, I have an idea!" cried Harry eagerly.

"Well, Harry, out with it."

"We can put the nugget in the trunk."

There was an old trunk, covered with hair, which had been left by the last occupant of the cabin. The lock was broken, and it was not of much use or value, but the boys occasionally used it as a seat.

"What security would that be?" said Obed. "It is easy enough to open the trunk."

"I know it, but I have another idea. Wrap up that stone in the handkerchief in place of the nugget. The thief—if one should come—would see it, and make off with it without stopping to examine its contents."

Obed smiled grimly.

"That's a good idea," he said. "I believe you're right, boy. It's dark, and the thief couldn't tell the difference till he came to examine it."

Stones and fragments of rock are rare in that part of Australia, and I am not prepared to explain how this particular rock found its way into the mining village. The boys had found it, however, and thinking it might be of some use had carried it to the cabin. Never, however, in their wildest imaginings had it entered into their minds to conceive the use to which they were now putting it.

No sooner said than done. The nugget was taken from the enfolding bandanna and dropped into the trunk, which Obed placed at the head of his pallet.

"I wish there was a lock and key," he said. "I should somehow feel safer."

"It's no use wishing," said Harry. "We've got to take things as we find them."

"That's true philosophy, boy. Now get the rock and tie it up."

Harry did so.

"Where shall I put it?" he asked.

"Anywhere where it can be seen easily. We won't trouble the thief to look round much. We'll make everything easy for him."

When the transfer was effected, the boys laughed with glee.

"Do you know, Obed," said Harry, "I shall be rather disappointed now if the thief doesn't come."

"I can get along without him," said Obed dryly.

"But it'll be such a good joke, Obed."

"I don't care so much about jokes as I did when I was your age, Harry. I used to be a great feller for jokes when I was along in my teens. Did I ever tell you the joke I played on the schoolmaster?

"Well, I was attendin' the district school the winter I was sixteen, and I expect I was rather troublesome, though there wasn't anything downright bad about me. But I remember one day when I stuck a bent pin in the chair the master usually sat in, and I shan't forget till my dyin' day how quick he riz up when he sat down in it."

Obed chuckled at the recollection, and so did the boys. Their sympathies ought to have been with the schoolmaster, but I am sorry to say that did not prevent their enjoying the joke.

"Were you found out?" asked Jack.

"Not exactly, but I think the master always suspected me. At any rate he was always cuffin' me and pullin' my hair. I didn't mind the fust so much as the last. So one day I got my mother to cut my hair close to my head. When I went to school the master gave me a queer look. He knew what made me have my hair cut. The next time I got into mischief he called me up, and instead of pullin' my hair he pulled my ears till I hollered. 'Now go home and get your ears cut off,' he said, but I didn't."

"It seems to me the joke was on you that time, Obed."

"I've surmised as much myself," said Obed, laughing quietly. "But I'm tired, boys, and I believe I shall have to go off to sleep, nugget or no nugget."

"All right! Good-night, Obed."

"Good-night, boys."

The thief had little difficulty in entering the cabin. No one in the mining settlement thought of locking the outer door or closing the windows. In many cases the door was left ajar; in some cases there were none. It was not necessary, therefore, to become a housebreaker. Entrance then was the least difficulty.

The tramp, however, was not quite easy in his mind. He didn't care for the two boys, but he glanced with apprehension at the reclining figure of the tall gaunt Yankee, who was thin but wiry, and possessed of more than ordinary physical strength.

"If he should tackle me," thought the midnight visitor with a shudder, "it would be all up with me. He could shake the life out of me."

But the stake was a valuable one—it would in all probability make him comfortable for life, if judiciously husbanded—and Obed's slumber seemed so profound that there appeared to be no risk. Nevertheless the tramp trembled, and his heart was in his mouth as he stealthily got in through the open window, and moved towards the nugget, or what he supposed to be such. He had one eye on Obed as he reached for the bundle. It was with difficulty that he could lift it, so heavy was it, but this only encouraged him, and made his eyes sparkle covetously. The heavier it was, the more valuable it must be. Were it twice as heavy he would be willing to carry it ten miles, enduring cheerfully all the fatigue it might entail. No thought of the rightful owners or of their disappointment disturbed him. That greed of gain which hardens the heart and banishes all scruples held firm dominion over him.

He lifted the bundle, and as noiselessly as he entered he made his egress through the window.

He thought he was unobserved, but he was mistaken.

Harry Vane was usually a heavy sleeper, but the thought of the nugget, even in his sleeping hours, weighed upon him and entered into his dreams. Singularly, he was dreaming at this very moment that it was being stolen, and in the intensity of his excitement all at once he became broad awake, just as the thief was disappearing through the window. With a startled look he glanced toward the place where the false nugget had been placed.

It was gone!

Evidently the thief had been taken in, and the thought amused him so much that he almost unconsciously laughed aloud. The sound fell on the ears of the receding thief, and filled his heart with apprehension, though he fancied it was a sound emitted in sleep. Still, it might precede awakening.

Once out of the window he did not stand upon the order of his going, but fled with a speed remarkable considering the weight of the bundle he carried.

Harry rose from his bed, and though he felt sure the thief had been deceived, he still, in order to make sure, opened the trunk and felt for the lump of gold. With a thrill of joy he found it still there. Then he could give way to his sense of amusement, and laughed long and loud. He did not, however, arouse Jack and Obed, who, like himself, were sound sleepers. He didn't like, however, to have all the amusement to himself, so he shook the Yankee till he awoke.

"What's the matter?" asked Obed, in a drowsy tone.

"We've been robbed," answered Harry.

"What!" exclaimed Mr. Stackpole in dismay, bounding from his pallet, now thoroughly awake. "What is that you say?"

"The nugget is gone!" said Harry.

"Confusion!" ejaculated Obed. "When? Who took it?"

"Don't be alarmed, Obed," said Harry quietly. "It's only the bogus nugget. The real one is safe where we hid it."

"Tell me all about it, Harry. What skunk has been in here?"

"You know—the man that was spying about our claim—the tramp."

"Did you see him?"

"Not till he was just getting out of the window!"

Harry recounted briefly his sudden awakening, and the sight that greeted him as he opened his eyes.

"I wish I'd been awake. I'd have boosted him out of that window," said Obed grimly.

"I have no doubt you would, Obed," said Harry laughing, "but I think we needn't feel much of a grudge against the poor fellow. When he comes to examine his booty by daylight, it's my impression he'll feel sick enough."

Obed laughed to. "I'd like to be looking on when he makes the discovery," he said. "He'll look green enough, I guess."

"How could the fellow have found out that we had found it?" said Harry, with a puzzled expression.

"He must have been out late and seen us coming from the mine."

"It is lucky we thought of hiding it, and leaving the rock in its place, Obed."

"That's so. The rock came in handy for once."

"Do you think there is any danger of another visit to-night?"

"No; he probably won't discover how he has been tricked till morning."

"And even if he does he may suppose that this rock is what we brought with us."

"Possibly. Still, Harry, I think we'd better keep awake and watch to-night. It will only be for one night, as to-morrow we can make arrangements to send the nugget by express to Melbourne."

"I thought we should be carrying it there ourselves."

"No, it would not be safe. To-morrow everybody will know that we have found a nugget, and if we attempted to carry it ourselves we should not get ten miles away without being attacked, and perhaps killed."

"Then we can send it by express?" queried Harry.

"Yes, I have inquired into this—not that I thought we would be lucky enough to need the information. The government escorts charge one per cent., and besides the Crown exacts a royalty of ten per cent."

"That's pretty steep, isn't it, Obed?"

"I will cheerfully bear my part of it," said Obed. "I remember there was an old fellow in our place who owned considerable property—at any rate he was taxed for fifteen thousand dollars. Whenever taxes became due he was always groanin' and predictin' that he'd end his days in the poorhouse. My father, who was only taxed for fifteen hundred, said to him one day, 'Mr. Higgins, if you'll give me half of your property, I'll agree to pay taxes on the whole, so that you'll have nothing to pay.'"

"Did he accept?" asked Harry, with a smile.

"Not much, but he stopped growlin'. It may have given him a new idea of the matter."

"How soon do you think of getting away, Obed?"

"As soon as we have sold the claim," answered the Yankee. "When it gets reported round the camp what we've found there'll be plenty that'll want to buy it on speculation, you may be sure of that."

"I didn't think of that," said Harry, his eyes brightening. "We're luckier than I thought."

"Yes," answered Obed jocularly, "we're men of property now. I'm afraid we'll have to pay taxes ourselves when we get home."

CHAPTER XIII
A THIEF'S EMBARRASSMENT

HEN the thief left Obed Stackpole's cabin with his booty his heart was filled with exultation. He had been drifting about for years, the football of fortune, oftener down than up, and had more than once known what it was to pass an entire day without food. And all this because he had never been willing to settle down to steady work or honest industry. He had set out in life with a dislike for each, and a decided preference for living by his wits. Theft was no new thing for him. Once he had barely escaped with his life in one of the Western States of America for stealing a horse. He had drifted to Australia, with no idea of working at the mines or anywhere else, but with the intention of robbing some lucky miner and making off with the proceeds of his industry.

Now, he had succeeded, and his heart was light.

"No more hard work for me," he said to himself joyfully, "no more privation and suffering. Now I can live like a gentleman."

It never seemed to occur to him that a thief could by no possibility live like a gentleman. To be a gentleman, in his opinion, meant having a pocketful of money.

He would like to have examined the nugget, but there was no time, nor was there light enough to form an opinion of it. Besides, Obed and the two boys might at any moment discover their loss, and then there would be pursuers on his track. He could not hide it, for it was too large, and any one seeing what he carried would suspect its nature and character.

The responsibility of property was upon him now. It was an unaccustomed sensation. This thief began now to dread an encounter with other thieves. There were other men, as well as himself, who had little respect for the rights of property, and this he well knew.

"Where shall I go?" he asked himself in perplexity.

It would not do to stay in the neighbourhood of the mining camp. By dawn, or as soon as tidings of the robbery should spread, there would be an organised pursuit. In any mining settlement a thief fares hard. In the absence of any established code of laws, the relentless laws of Judge Lynch are executed with merciless severity. Beads of perspiration began to form on the brow of the thief as he realised the terrible danger he had incurred. What good would it do him after all to get away with the nugget if it should cost him his life, and that was a contingency, as his experience assured him, by no means improbable.

"If I were only in Melbourne," he said to himself, "I would lose no time in disposing of the nugget, and then would take the first ship for England—or anywhere else. Any place would be better than Australia, for that will soon be too hot to hold me."

It was one thing to wish, and another to realise the wish. He was still in the immediate vicinity of the mining camp, and there were almost insuperable difficulties in the way of getting far from it with his treasure safe.

The thief kept on his way, however, and after a while reached a piece of woods.

"This will be a good place to hide," he bethought himself. "I may be able to conceal the nugget somewhere."

His first feeling of exultation had given place to one of deep anxiety and perplexity. After, he was not as happy as he anticipated. Only yesterday he had been poor—almost destitute—but at any rate free from anxiety and alarm. Now he was rich, or thought he was, and his heart was filled with nervous apprehension.

He wandered about for two or three hours, weary and feeling great need of sleep, but afraid to yield to the impulse. Suppose he should lose consciousness, and sleep till morning: the first man who found him asleep would rob him of the precious nugget, and then he would be back again where he had been the day before, and for years back. The dream of his life had been fulfilled, and he was in no position to enjoy it. Oftentimes God grants our wishes only to show us how little they add to our happiness.

At last he saw before him a cabin—deserted, apparently. It would afford him a place to obtain needed repose, and there would be some means of hiding his rich treasure.

He peered timidly into the cabin and found it empty. On the floor in the corner was a pallet. He put the nugget under the upper part, thus raising it and supplying the place of a pillow. It was hard enough, as the reader will imagine, but it was better than nothing, and appeared to combine safety with a chance to rest.

The thief fell asleep, and slept soundly. When he awoke it was bright, and the morning was evidently well advanced. In an instant consciousness came, and with anxious thought he felt for the nugget. It was still there, as he realised joyfully. He was on the point of examining the nugget, when a step was heard. He looked up startled, and saw a man entering the cabin. This man was such another as himself—an adventurer—and the tramp remembered to have seen him about the camp.

"Halloa!" the new arrival said, gazing with a little surprise at the prostrate man.

"Halloa!" returned the other, surveying the new arrival with apprehension.

"Is this your crib?"

"No, I'm only passing the night here."

"Haven't I seen you at the mines?"

"Yes, I have been there."

"And now you are leaving, are you?"

"I haven't made up my mind. I don't know. I want to get away for one thing."

"So do I. Suppose we keep company, friend. Two are more social than one, eh?"

This proposal gave the first man anxious thought. If he had a companion, he could not hide for any length of time the fact that he was in possession of the nugget. Yet he did not know how to refuse without exciting suspicion. The new arrival noticed it, and it stirred up anger in him.

"Perhaps I ain't good enough for you?" he added, frowning.

"No, no, it isn't that," said the first eagerly.

"Don't you want me to go with you?" demanded the new arrival bluntly. "Yes or no."

"Have you got any money?" asked the thief, "because I haven't."

"No more have I. We'll be equal partners."

"Then I'm afraid we won't get very far."

"You'll get as far as I will. But I say, what is that under your head, pard?"

The question had come at last. The thief trembled and answered nervously:

"It's—it's—I am using it for a pillow," he faltered.

"Let us see your pillow," said the new arrival suspiciously.

The thief came to a sudden determination, suggested by necessity. Two would make a stronger guard than one, and, though this man was not the one he would have selected, accident had thrown them together, and he would risk it.

"Look here, my friend," he said, "it's a great secret."

"Oh, a secret, is it?"

"Yes, but I am going to make you my confidant. I am greatly in need of a friend and partner, and I'll make it worth your while to stand by me. I'll give you a quarter of—what I have here—if you'll see me safe to Melbourne."

"What is it, pard? Out with it, quick!"

"It's—a nugget, and the biggest one that's been found at Bendigo since they commenced mining."

"A nugget! Great Jehoshaphat! Let me see it!"

The thief drew the bundle—still wrapped in Obed's red bandanna—from underneath the pallet, while his companion in intense excitement bent over to catch a glimpse of the treasure.

CHAPTER XIV
BAFFLED CUPIDITY

N expression of surprise and dismay, almost ludicrous, appeared on the faces of the two adventurers as the contents of the handkerchief were revealed.

"Why, it's nothing but a rock!" exclaimed the new-comer, with an oath.

The thief stared at him in helpless consternation, and was unable to utter a word.

"What does all this mean?" asked the new-comer sternly. "If you are humbugging me, I'll——" and he finished the sentence with an oath.

"I don't know what it means," answered the thief, in a disconsolate tone. "I'm just as much surprised as you are."

"Where did you get it? How came you to make such a fool of yourself?" demanded the new-comer, frowning heavily.

"You know that Yankee and the two boys who have a claim next to Pickett's?"

"Well?"

"Last night I was coming from the Hut"—that was the local name of the cabin devoted to gambling purposes—"when I saw them coming from their claim. The Yankee had this—rock tied up in yonder handkerchief. Of course, I supposed it was a nugget. No one would suppose he was taking all that pains with a common rock."

"Go on! Did you follow them?"

"Yes; that is, I kept them in sight. They entered their cabin, and I waited, perhaps three-quarters of an hour, till they had time to fall asleep."

"Were you near the cabin all the time?"

"No; I didn't care to be too near for fear I should be observed. I wanted the nugget, but I didn't want to run any risk."

"I have no doubt you were very prudent," said the second, with an unpleasant sneer. Doubtless he would have done the same, but his disappointment was so great that he could not resist the temptation of indulging in this fling at the man who had unintentionally contributed to it.

"Of course I was," said the first, with some indignation. "Would you have had me enter the cabin while they were all awake, and carry it off under their very eyes? That would be mighty sensible."

"At any rate, then you would have got the genuine nugget."

"What do you mean? Do you think there was a nugget?"

"Of course I do. It's as plain as the nose on your face, and that's plain enough, in all conscience. They've played a trick on you."

"What trick?"

"It appears to me that you are mighty stupid, my friend. They hid away the real nugget, and put this in its place. That Yankee is a good deal sharper than you are, and he wasn't going to run no risks."

"Do you believe this?" asked the thief, his jaw falling.

"There's no doubt of it. They've had a fine laugh at you before this, I'll be bound."

"Just my luck!" ejaculated the thief dolefully. "After all the pains I've taken, too."

"Yes, it is hard lines on a poor industrious man like you!" said the new-comer cynically. "You're not smart enough to be a successful thief."

"I suppose you are," retorted the other resentfully.

"Yes, I flatter myself I am," returned the other composedly. "When I take anything, at any rate I have the sense to take something worth carrying away—not a worthless rock like this. You must have had a fine time lugging it from the mines."

"It nearly broke my back," said the thief gloomily.

"And now you don't know what to do with it? Take my advice, my friend, and carry it back to the original owner. He may find it handy another time."

"I'll be blessed if I do," growled the unhappy thief.

"I doubt that," said his companion dryly. "However, do as you please. It don't interest me. I don't think on the whole I will accept your offer of a partnership. When I take a partner I want a man with some small supply of brains."

The first looked at him resentfully. He did not like these taunts, and would have assaulted him had he dared, but the new-comer was powerfully built, and evidently an unsafe man to take liberties with. He threw himself back on the pallet and groaned.

"Well," said the second after a pause, "when you've got through crying over spilt milk, will you kindly tell me where I can get something to eat?"

"I don't know."

"Humph! that's short and to the point. It is something I would like very much to know, for my part. I feel decidedly hungry."

"I have no appetite," said the luckless thief mournfully.

"You will have, after a while. Then you can't think of any cabin near by where we could get a breakfast?"

"There's Joe's."

"Are you acquainted with Joe?"

"Yes."

"Is your credit good with him?"

"I think he would trust me for a breakfast."

"And me? You can introduce me as a friend of yours."

"You haven't been talking like a friend of mine," said the first resentfully.

"Perhaps not. However, you must make allowances for my natural disappointment. You led me into it, you know."

"If it comes to that, I have done you no harm. Even if the nugget wasn't real, you had no claim to it."

"You excited my hopes, and that's enough to rile any man—that is, when disappointment follows. However, there's no use crying over spilt milk. I have an idea that may lead to something."

"What is it?" asked the thief, with some eagerness.

"I will tell you—after breakfast. My ideas don't flow freely when I am hungry. Come, my friend, get up, and lead the way to Joe's. I have an aching void within, which needs filling up. Your appetite may come too—after a walk."

Somehow this man, cool and cynical as he was, impressed his fellow adventurer, and he rose obediently, and led the way.

"I wish I knew what was your idea," he said.

"Well, I don't mind telling you. I believe the Yankee did find a nugget."

"Well?"

"You haven't got it, but you may get it—that is, we may get it."

"I don't see how. He will be on his guard now."

"Of course he will. I don't mean that we should repeat the blunder of last night. You may be sure he won't keep it in his cabin another night."

"Then how are we to get it?"

"Follow him to Melbourne. He'll carry it there, and on the way we can relieve him of it."

"There's something in that."

"We shall be together, and he won't take me in as readily as he did you. After breakfast, if we are lucky enough to get any, we must go back to the camp, and find out what we can about his plans. Do you think any one saw you last night when you were in the cabin?"

"No."

"That is well. Then you won't be suspected. But I can't say a word more till I have had breakfast."

After half-an-hour's walking—it was only half a mile, but the soil was boggy, rendering locomotion difficult—they reached a humble wayside cabin, which was in some sort a restaurant, and by dint of diplomacy and a promise of speedy payment, they secured a meal to which, despite their disappointment, they did ample justice.

Breakfast over, they resumed their fatiguing walk, and reached the mining camp about ten o'clock.

Fatigued by their exertions of the previous days and the late hours they had kept, Obed and the boys rose at a later hour than usual. About eight o'clock Obed opened his eyes, and noticed that his two young companions were fast asleep.

"It's time to get up, boys," he said, giving them a gentle shake.

The boys opened their eyes, and realised, by the bright sunshine entering the cabin, that the day was already well advanced.

"What time is it, Obed?" asked Harry.

"Past eight o'clock. We shall be late at our work."

He smiled, and his smile was reflected on the faces of the boys. Their success of the day before made it a matter of indifference whether they accomplished a good day's work or not.

"What are we going to do about the nugget, Obed?" asked Harry.

"After breakfast we will carry it to the office of the commissioner, and get his receipt for it."

"I shall be glad to get it out of our hands," said Jack.

"If that is the case, Jack, suppose you give your share to me," said Harry, in joke.

"I didn't mean to get rid of it in that way," said the young sailor.

"You would be as ready to give it as I to accept it," said Harry. "No, Jack, I want you to have your share. I am sure you will have a use for it."

After breakfast the three emerged from the cabin, bearing the precious nugget with them. They did not meet any one on their way to the office of the commissioner, for all the miners had gone to their work. This suited them, for until they had disposed of the nugget, they did not care to have their good luck made public.

The royal commissioner was a stout Englishman with a red face and abundant whiskers of the same colour. He chanced to be at the door of the office as the party appeared.

"Well, can I do anything for you?" he asked.

"Yes, sir; you can give us a receipt for this nugget."

"Nugget!" ejaculated the commissioner, fixing his eyes on the burden which Mr. Stackpole carried. "You don't mean to say that you have found a nugget of that size!"

"That's just what we've done," answered Obed.

"When did you find it?"

"Well, we took it from the mine about midnight. We found it in the afternoon, but calculated we'd better take possession when there wasn't so many lookin' on. I say, Mr. Commissioner, I don't think it would agree with me to be a rich man. I got broken of my rest last night, from havin' the nugget in the cabin."

"You ran very little risk. No one could have found out that you had it in your possession," remarked the commissioner.

"That's where you are mistaken, commissioner. We came near being robbed of it only an hour after we brought it home."

"Bless my soul! How did that happen?"

"A pesky thief sneaked in, and carried it off, as he thought."

"How could he think he carried it off when he did not?"

Upon this Obed explained the trick to which he had resorted, and the commissioner laughed heartily.

"Do you know the man—the thief, I mean?" he asked.

"Yes, it is a man that has been prowlin' round the camp for some weeks, not doin' anything, but watchin' for a chance to appropriate the property of some lucky miner. I'd like to see the fellow's face when he opens the handkerchief this morning, and finds the rock."

"It appears you have lost a handkerchief, at any rate," said the commissioner, with a smile.

"He's welcome to it," answered Obed, "if it will comfort him any. I brought it away from home two years ago, and now I can afford to buy another."

By this time the nugget had been carried into the office and exposed to view.

"It is a splendid specimen," said the commissioner admiringly. "It is certainly the largest that has been found in this camp."

"Have any been found before?" asked Harry.

"Yes; six months ago a Scotch miner named Lindsay found one weighing twenty-two pounds and some ounces."

"Is he here now?"

"Yes, and without a shilling."

"Didn't his nugget benefit him any then?" asked Harry.

"It became a curse to him. He obtained some hundreds of pounds for it, and all went in three months."

"How did he get rid of it?"

"In drinking and gambling. Two months since he drifted back to the camp in rags. He did not have money enough to buy a claim, but being a good practical miner he got a chance to work a claim on shares for another man, who had just come out from Melbourne, and who knew very little of mining. I hope you will make better use of your money. Are these boys your partners?"

"Yes, Mr. Commissioner, they are equal partners. What's one's luck, is the luck of all."

The commissioner then weighed the nugget, the three awaiting the result with great interest.

"It weighs seventy-four pounds and four ounces," he announced. "My friend, it will be famous in the annals of Australia. If I am not mistaken, when it is known it will create a stampede to our mines."

"About how much do you think it will realise?" asked Obed.

"At a rough guess, I should say three thousand pounds. It may be more and it may be less."

Obed Stackpole's rough face was fairly radiant.

"I say, boys," he remarked, turning to Harry and Jack, "that's a pretty good day's work, isn't it?"

"I should say so, Obed."

The commissioner made out a receipt, which Obed put away carefully in his pocket.

"That's better than carrying the nugget round," he said.

"I suppose you will go to Melbourne," said the commissioner.

"Yes, we shall start in a day or two."

Here Obed paused, for it occurred to him that there were practical difficulties in the way of carrying out his plan.

"That is," he added slowly, "if we can raise the money. I suppose we can't borrow on the nugget?"

"No, but I can suggest a way out of your difficulties. You can sell your claim. It will realise a good round sum, as the one from which the nugget has been taken."

"That's so, Mr. Commissioner. Thank you for the suggestion. Boys, there is still some business before us. We'll realise something extra, it seems. I don't care how much, if it's only enough to take us to Melbourne."

Just then a miner entered the office, and, seeing the nugget, instantly made it his purpose to report the lucky find throughout the camp. The effect was instant and electrical. Every miner stopped work, and there was a rush to the commissioner's office to see the nugget. All were cheered up. If there was one nugget, there must be more. Confidence was restored to many who had been desponding. Obed and the two boys were the heroes of the hour, and the crowd came near lifting them on their shoulders, and bearing them off in triumph.

Obed felt that this was a good time to sell the claim.

"Boys," he said, "we struck it rich and no mistake. How rich I don't know. There may be other nuggets where this came from. But I and my partners want to go back home. The claim's for sale. Who wants it?"

CHAPTER XV
SELLING THE CLAIM

"LET'S adjourn to the mine," said Tom Lewis, a short, sturdy Englishman.

"Yes, let's see the place where the nugget was found," echoed another.

"All right! I'm agreeable," said Obed.

Followed by a crowd of miners, Obed Stackpole strode to the claim where he had "struck it rich." In spite of his homely face and ungainly form there was more than one who would have been willing to stand in his shoes, homeliness and all. The day before little notice was taken of him. Now he was a man who had won fame at a bound.

They soon stood around the lucky claim.

"It isn't much to look at, gentlemen," said Obed, "but looks is deceptive, as my old grandmother used to tell me. 'Handsome is as handsome does,' and this 'ere hole's done the handsome thing for me and my partners, and I venture to say it hasn't got through doin' handsome things. It's made three of us rich, and it's ready to make somebody else rich. Who'll be the lucky man? Do I hear a bid?"

"Fifty pounds," said Tom Lewis.

"That'll do to start on, but it won't do to take. Fifty pounds I am offered. Who says a hundred?"

A German miner offered a hundred, and Tom Lewis raised ten pounds.

A Scotch miner, Aleck Graham, offered a hundred and twenty-five.

From that time the bids rose slowly. Obed showed himself an excellent auctioneer—indeed he had had some experience at home—and by his dry and droll remarks stimulated the bidding when it became dull, and did not declare the claim sold till it was clear no higher bid could be obtained.

"Three hundred pounds, and sold to Frank Scott," he concluded. "Mr. Scott, I congratulate you. I calculate you've made a pretty good investment, and I shouldn't wonder if you'd find another nugget within a week. 'Birds of a feather flock together,' as my writing-book says, and 'it never rains but it pours.'"

Frank Scott came forward and made arrangements for the payment of the sum he had offered. Within five minutes he was offered an advance of twenty-five pounds for his bargain, which put him in good humour, though he declined it. I may as well say here, since we are soon to say farewell to Bendigo, that the claim yielded him double the amount of his investment, and though this was not up to his expectations, he had no reason to regret his purchase.

The little crowd of miners were just separating when two newcomers appeared on the scene. They were the well-matched pair who had met earlier in the morning at the deserted cabin. For convenience' sake we will call them Colson and Ropes, the former being the man who had stolen the nugget, as he supposed.

"What's all this crowd?" said Colson, in a tone of curiosity.

Ropes put the question to Tom Lewis, who chanced to be passing.

"Haven't you heard about the nugget?" asked Lewis.

"What nugget?" asked Colson innocently.

"That slab-sided Yankee, Obed Stackpole, found a nugget last night—a regular monster—and he's been selling his claim. I bid for it, but I didn't bid high enough."

"Where's the nugget?" asked Colson eagerly.

"In charge of the commissioner, who will send it under escort to Melbourne."

Colson expected this intelligence. Still he looked downcast. The chance of getting hold of it under such circumstances seemed very small.

"What did the claim go for?" questioned Ropes.

"Three hundred pounds. Frank Scott bought it."

"That's a pretty steep price."

"Yes, but there may be another nugget."

"And there may not."

"Then he'll be a loser. Of course there's a risk."

"Is the Yankee going to stay around here?" asked Colson.

"No; he and the two boys are going to Melbourne. I believe they are going back home."

"It's a shame that such a prize should go to Americans," said Colson, in a discontented tone.

He would have been very glad to head a movement for robbing Obed and the boys of the proceeds of their lucky discovery on this flimsy ground. But Tom Lewis was a fair-minded man.

"I don't see what that has to do with it," said he. "They found it, and they have a right to it. Of course, I'd rather it had been me; but it wasn't, and there's an end of it."

"Some people are born lucky!" grumbled Colson, as Lewis walked away. "I never had any luck."

"The nugget you found wasn't quite so valuable," returned Ropes grimly.

"No; I tugged away for nothing. My arms and shoulders are stiff enough this morning. And now the nugget is out of our reach."

"But not the three hundred pounds," said Ropes significantly.

"The price of the claim?"

"Yes."

"That's true, but it won't do us any good."

"The Yankee will carry that with him. It's worth trying for."

The suggestion seemed to strike Colson favourably. The two held a whispered consultation, which seemed to yield mutual satisfaction. They were, indeed, congenial spirits, and agreed upon one point, that it was better to make a living by knavery than by doing honest work for honest wages. Yet there is no harder or more unsatisfactory way of living than this. Ill-gotten gains seldom benefit the possessor, and the plans of wicked men often fail altogether.

Gradually the two had drawn near to the claim, and at last drew the attention of Obed and the boys.

Obed's thin face lighted up with satisfaction as he recognised the man who had attempted to steal the nugget.

"Good-mornin', squire," he said politely. "You look kind of tired, as if you was up late last night."

Colson eyed him sharply. "Does he suspect?" thought he. "Yes," he answered, in an indifferent tone, "I didn't rest very well."

"Where did you pass the night?"

"'Round here," he answered vaguely.

"You look as if you had been taking a long walk."

"You are very observing," said Colson, not over pleased.

"I always was. It pays a man—sometimes."

"I hear you've struck it rich," said Colson, not caring to take notice of the other's significant tone.

"Found a nugget, they tell me," interpolated Ropes. "How big was it?"

"Weighs about seventy-five pounds!"

"That is luck!" said Colson, with a sickly smile. He could scarcely help groaning as he thought of his loss.

"Well, yes, it is tolerable fortunate. I reckon me and the boys will be able to take it easy for a few years. But we came near losin' it, after all."

"How's that?" Colson asked, but he did not venture to meet Obed's glance.

"Some skunk saw us bringin' back the nugget, and prowled round till he thought we was all asleep. Then he got into the cabin and carried it off. That is, he thought he did, but we was a little too sharp for him. We tied up a big rock in my handkerchief, and I guess he had a sweet time carryin' it off."

"Ha! ha! A good joke!" said Colson, but his laughter was mirthless.

"I thought you'd enjoy the joke, squire," said Obed. "How I pity the poor fellow! His arms must ache with luggin' the old rock. The best of it is we know the fellow that took it."

"You do?" ejaculated Colson, his jaw dropping.

"Yes; Harry woke up just in the nick of time and saw him scootin' out of the cabin. If I should tell the boys 'round here, I reckon they'd lynch him!" added Obed quietly.

"Just so," assented Colson, but his face was of a sickly hue, and taking Ropes by the arm he hurried him away.

"That fellow's well scared," said Obed, turning to his two young companions. "I reckon he'll make himself scarce till we're out of the way."

Obed and the boys made arrangements to travel with the party sent by the commissioner as an escort to the nugget and other sums entrusted to it by different miners. The strong guard gave them a sense of security which they would not have had under other circumstances.

They were all in high spirits. They were no longer penniless adventurers, but, though not rich, were possessed of enough gold to make them feel so. Now that they were well fixed they were all filled with a strong desire to see their home across the sea.

"I suppose, Obed, you'll be getting married soon after you reach home?" said Harry.

"The very first thing I shall do will be to pay off the mortgage on dad's farm," said Mr. Stackpole. "I want to see him a free man, with a home that can't be taken from him. Then I'll look after the other matter."

"You are right, Obed. I only wish I had a father to help and care for," said Harry soberly.

"I've got a stepfather," said Jack, "but I don't feel much like helping him."

"You have a mother, Jack."

"Yes, but I shall have to be careful about giving her money, for her husband would get it away from her before long."

"Well, boys, we won't borrow trouble before the time comes. For all I know Suke Stanwood may have got tired of waitin' for me, and married some other feller."

"In that case, Obed, I suppose you would die of a broken heart."

"Not much, but I don't mind sayin' that I should feel uncommon blue."

Two days elapsed before Obed and his party started on their return trip. Meanwhile Colson and Ropes had disappeared. The boys had expected to see them about the camp, but they had vanished.

"I wonder what has become of them?" said Harry, just as they were starting.

"I reckon they're hatchin' some new mischief, wherever they are," returned Obed composedly. "You may be sure they're not engaged in any honest work."

"Perhaps Colson is trying to sell his nugget," suggested Jack with a smile.

"He's welcome to all he can get for it," said Obed.

Obed was very near the truth in his conjecture. Their greed was excited by thoughts of the nugget which our three friends had discovered, and their brains were busied with plans for obtaining possession of it. The chances didn't seem very encouraging. It was under strong escort, and it would be sheer madness for the two to attack an armed party. It would require a much larger force than they could command to make an attack at all practicable.

With no special plans, but with the hope that something would turn up in their favour, the two men started for Melbourne in advance of the government party. They were indebted for the requisite funds to a successful theft by Colson, who was an expert in his line. It is unnecessary to chronicle their daily progress. We will look in upon them on the fourth day.

They were making toilsome progress over the boggy road, when all at once they were confronted by three bushrangers headed by Fletcher.

"Surrender, or you are dead men!" exclaimed Fletcher, with a boldness which will be easily understood when it is considered that his force outnumbered the travellers two to one.

Neither Colson nor Ropes appeared to be frightened. Indeed, they were looking for such an encounter.

"All right, gentlemen," said Ropes quietly. "We are quite ready to surrender."

"Empty your pockets," was the next order.

"All right again!" said Ropes. "I am sorry to say we haven't much to surrender."

"Is this all you have?" asked Fletcher, frowning when a pound and ten shillings were delivered to him as their united contributions to the bushrangers' fund.

"We haven't a penny more."

"Search them!" said Fletcher to his followers.

A search, however, failed to bring to light anything more.

"Why, you poor tramps!" exclaimed Fletcher in disgust. "You are unworthy the attention of gentlemen."

"Perhaps not, captain," replied Colson. "May I have a word with you in private?"

Not without suspicion Fletcher granted this unexpected request, and stepped aside with Colson a few paces, taking care, however, to keep near enough to his party to insure his safety.

"Well, what have you to say?" he asked abruptly.

"I have no money to give you," replied Colson, "but I have information that will enable you to obtain a great deal."

"What is your object in telling me this?" demanded Fletcher, still suspiciously.

"The fact is, my friend and I want to join with you in the enterprise, and get a fair share of the booty."

"Do you wish to join our band, then?"

"Well, not permanently, but for a little while."

"Out with the information, then!"

"Will you agree to our terms?"

"What are they?"

"We want half of the prize."

"You are very modest," said Fletcher, in a sarcastic tone. "How much will it amount to?"

"Not far from twenty thousand pounds."

Fletcher pricked up his ears. This was indeed a prize worth trying for.

"Give particulars," he said.

"A big nugget is on the way to Melbourne, or will be in a day or two. It was found at Bendigo. I don't know how much it will net, but probably seventy-five thousand dollars. Then there is a considerable amount of dust besides."

"Who is to carry it? Is it in the hands of a private party?"

"No, it is under government escort."

Fletcher's countenance changed.

"That is a different matter," he said. "There is danger in attacking a government party."

"Think of the big sum at stake."

"It would require the co-operation of the whole band."

"Suppose it does."

"There will be more to divide it among. The captain would not agree for a moment to give away half."

"Say a third, then."

"I am not authorised to make any bargain. That will be for the captain to decide. You had better tell me all you know about it, and I will lay it before the captain and secure you the best terms I can on conditions——"

"Well?"

"That you give me quarter of your share."

"That is unreasonable," said Colson, disappointed.

"Then go ahead and rob the government train yourself."

Colson saw that he was helpless, and must submit to any terms proposed. He accordingly signified his assent.

"Very well, then," said Fletcher, "you may come with us, and I will introduce you to the captain. By the way, who found the nugget? You have not told me that."

"A Yankee and two boys."

"What was the Yankee's name?" asked Fletcher eagerly.

"Stackpole—Obed Stackpole."

Fletcher whistled.

"I know the man," he said. "The boys are about sixteen—one a sailor?"

"Yes."

"I know them all, and I owe them all a grudge. There is nothing I should like better than to take all they have and leave them penniless."

"I don't like them myself," said Colson, thinking this was the way to curry favour with his new acquaintance.

"You know them also?"

"Yes; they have treated me meanly."

Colson probably referred to their substituting a common rock for the rich nugget, and so subjecting him to mortification and disappointment.

Fletcher asked him a few more questions, and then with the new accessions plunged into the woods, and led his party to the headquarters of the bushrangers.

CHAPTER XVI
TAKEN CAPTIVE

HE new recruits, on being introduced to the captain of the bushrangers, were subjected to a searching examination by the chief, a suspicion having arisen in his mind that the two were spies sent out by the government to lure the outlaws into a trap. He was convinced after a while that they were acting in good faith, and a conference was called to decide what should be done in the matter. On this point opinions differed. The nugget, of course, would be a valuable prize, but it would be impossible to dispose of it in Melbourne, as the fact of its discovery would have been published, and any person attempting to sell it would be instantly arrested. This view was held by Captain Ring himself.

"That objection is easily met," said Fletcher.

"In what way?"

"One of the band could be sent to England to dispose of it. He could carry it in his trunk as ordinary luggage."

"Perhaps you would like to undertake the commission," said Captain Ring.

"I should be very willing," said Fletcher eagerly.

"I don't doubt you would," returned the captain, in a sarcastic tone. "Who would insure your making over the proceeds to us?"

"I hope you don't doubt my integrity," said Fletcher, with an air of virtuous indignation.

"Perhaps I had better say nothing on that subject, Fletcher. The band are unwilling to subject you to the temptation—that's all. Many good men go wrong."

"You might send some one with me," suggested Fletcher, unwilling to give up the tempting prospect.

"We haven't got the nugget yet," answered the captain dryly.

Colson and Ropes had listened with interest to the discussion. They began to fear that nothing would be done. They would have been as much opposed as any one to trusting Fletcher, as he had not inspired them with confidence. It takes a rogue to detect a rogue, and they already suspected his true character. Colson's hope of revenge on Obed Stackpole seemed slipping through his fingers.

"The Yankee and the two boys have a good deal of gold about them," suggested Colson. "Of course it isn't much compared with the nugget, but it is better than nothing."

"How much has the Yankee?" demanded Ring.

"Three hundred pounds at least."

"That is something, but as he will travel with the government escort, we should have to attack the whole party."

"Not necessarily. I have a plan that I think will work."

"Detail it."

Colson did so. What it was will appear in due time.

Meanwhile Obed and the two boys had started on their way to Melbourne. With a strong military escort they gave themselves up to joyful anticipations of the bright future that opened before them. They no longer entertained apprehensions of being waylaid, being secure in the strength of their party.

They travelled by easy stages, and at night camped out. A sentry was always posted, who stood guard while the rest were asleep, for, unlikely as an attack might be, it was deemed necessary to provide against it.

Often, however, after supper Obed and the two boys would take a walk together, in order to talk over their plans without interruption from others. On the third evening they unwittingly walked a little further than usual. Harry was the first to notice it.

"Hadn't we better return, Obed?" he said. "We must be a mile from the camp."

"You are right," said Obed. "It would be rather unlucky to meet with the bushrangers, just as we are gettin' on so well."

"That's true; we mustn't run any risks."

They started to return, when Jack, stopping suddenly, said, "I thought I heard a groan."

"So did I," said Harry.

They paused, and the groan was repeated. It appeared to come from a little distance to the left in the recesses of the forest.

"If there's any poor critter in pain we ought to help him," said Obed. "Come along, boys!"

It was not difficult to discover the spot from which the groan proceeded. A man of middle age lay outstretched beneath a tree, with an expression of pain on his face.

"What's the matter, my friend?" asked Obed, standing over him.

"The bushrangers have robbed and beaten me," said the prostrate man feebly.

"You don't say so! How long since?"

"About an hour."

"Then they must be near by," said Harry.

"No; they went away as soon as they got my money."

Meanwhile Jack had been attentively examining the face of the alleged victim. He quietly beckoned to Harry to move off to a little distance.

"Well, Jack, what is it?" asked Harry, somewhat surprised.

"That man is one of the bushrangers. I remember his face very well. It is one of the gang that captured us."

Harry was naturally startled.

"Are you sure of this?" he asked.

"Yes, I know him as well as I do Obed."

"Then it is a plot. We must get away if we can. There is danger in staying here."

"You are right there, Harry."

"I will go up and take Obed's place while you call him away."

Harry advanced to the side of the victim, and said quietly, "Jack wishes to speak to you a moment, Obed. He thinks we can carry this gentleman with us, as he has lost all his money."

"Very well," said Obed, and walked to where Jack was standing.

Harry scrutinised the man's face, and he too recognised him as one of the gang—but his face did not betray his suspicions.

"Were you robbed of much money?" he asked, in a sympathising tone.

"I had the value of a hundred pounds with me," said the other feebly.

"I suppose you came from Bendigo like ourselves?"

"Yes; have you been lucky?"

"We had some luck, but we are tired of mining, and are going back to Melbourne. Would you like to have us take you along also?"

"Yes, if you would be so kind."

At this moment Obed's voice was heard.

"Come here, Harry; we'll make a litter to carry our friend there if he is unable to walk."

"All right, Obed."

There might have been something in Obed's voice that betrayed him. At any rate, the victim, looking up, eyed him keenly, and then, to the surprise of the boys, gave a sharp whistle. Their suspicions were at once kindled, and they started to run, but too late. From the underbrush there sprang out three bushrangers, accompanied by Colson and Ropes, who covered the boys with their weapons.

"Halt there!" exclaimed Fletcher, in a tone of authority.

"Oh, it's you, is it?" said Obed with apparent coolness, though his heart sank within him.

"Yes, it's I, Mr. Stackpole," returned Fletcher, with a grim smile. "I hope you're better fixed than when we met last. I hear you've found a nugget."

"One of those gentlemen with you can give you information about that," said Obed, indicating Colson.

Colson frowned and bit his lip.

"He has told us about it."

"Ask him for it then. He broke into our tent the night we found it and carried it off."

"Is this true?" demanded Fletcher, eyeing Colson suspiciously.

"No, it's a lie. The nugget is in charge of a mounted escort on the way to Melbourne."

"What have you done with *your* nugget, Colson?" asked Obed.

Colson did not reply.

"There's no time to waste here. Stackpole, you and the boys will have to go with us. Here, you two men, close behind them. We must not let them escape."

The party started with the captives in the middle. It was decidedly a bad outlook for our three friends.

It must be confessed that the reflections of Obed and the two boys were far from pleasant. The cup of happiness had been dashed from their lips just as they had begun to taste it. Then again it was very mortifying to watch the exultation of Fletcher and Colson, who had finally triumphed over them after being successfully baffled.

"The worst of it is," said Obed to Harry, who was walking alongside of him, "that them skunks have got the best of it. It's their time to crow now."

"That's the way I feel," said Harry soberly. "I believe I would rather have lost twice as much to anybody else."

"We haven't lost all, that's a comfort. They will take the money we have with us, but if ever we escape to Melbourne, there is the nugget money waiting for us."

Just then Colson stepped up with a smile on his face.

"It strikes me I've got about even with you, friend Stackpole," he said.

"Don't call me friend, Colson; I don't own any man as a friend who acts like you. So you're a bushranger, are you?"

"Certainly not," answered Colson, amazed.

"It looks like it," remarked Obed significantly.

"I am merely in the company of the bushrangers just at present."

"Aiding and abetting them in their scheming. That's so, isn't it?"

"No."

"You haven't any interest in the plunder, then?"

Now one of the bushrangers was within hearing, and Colson didn't venture to say "No," or it would be virtually giving up his share of the money taken from Obed and the boys.

"I don't care to answer any of your questions," he said stiffly.

"I don't wonder—not a mite, Colson. Still I'd like to ask one."

"What is it? I don't promise to answer it, though."

"Didn't you find that nugget rather heavy?" asked Obed slyly.

Colson didn't answer, but frowned, for the subject was a sore one.

"How many miles did you carry it, if I may be so bold?"

"I don't care to discuss the subject."

"I shouldn't if I were you. It makes me laugh when I think how you must have looked when you found out it was nothing but common rock."

"How much does it weigh?" inquired Colson, in a tone of curiosity.

"Somewhere between fifty and five hundred pounds. Are you thinking of attacking the guard? I wouldn't if I were you. They are prepared for gentlemen of your kind. You'd be more likely to carry off lead than gold."

"Confound the fellow!" thought Colson. "He looks as if he had the best of me—I must worry him a little."

"Do you know that you are in a very ticklish position?" he asked.

"I can't say it's a position I fancy much. Did you put our friends here on the track?"

"Yes, I did," answered Colson, in a tone of satisfaction.

"I thought so. That identifies you with them, Colson. You may find it used against you in a court of justice."

"I am no more a bushranger than you are," said Colson uneasily.

"I would respect you more if you was, Colson. They're open and aboveboard, anyway. You want to profit by the same means, but sneak out of it and say you're not a bushranger. It'll be hard to persuade the courts of that."

"I have nothing to do with courts."

"You may have yet. Let me give you a piece of advice."

"What is it?" demanded Colson suspiciously.

"Join the band permanently. You're a man after Fletcher's own heart. You and he will make a good match."

"Who is that mentioning my name?" asked Fletcher, who happened to be within hearing.

"I took that liberty, squire. I've been advisin' Colson here to join your band."

"What is that for?"

"I think it's a business that will suit him. His talents all lie in that direction. He'll be like a brother to you, Fletcher."

"What did he say?"

"He don't like the idea. He seems to feel above you. He says he is only keepin' company with you for a short time."

"Is that true?" demanded Fletcher, eyeing Colson with displeasure.

"I never said any such thing," said Colson eagerly. "He twists my words. I have the greatest respect for the bushrangers, whom I regard as gentlemen."

"Perhaps that is the reason you don't feel gratified to join them, Colson?"

Fletcher laughed at this palpable hit, but Colson looked annoyed.

"I don't expect to remain in this section of the country long," said Colson deprecatingly, for he was very much afraid of offending Fletcher. "Of course I can't form any permanent ties."

"It might be better for you to leave, Colson. I've an idee that it isn't good for your health to stay around here very long. You haven't made a shinin' success so far. Now, as to that nugget which you stole——"

"Do you mean to insult me? I never took any nugget."

"That's so. You're right there, Colson. But you thought you had, all the same. Fortunately, it's where you can't get at it."

"I have something to say on that point," said Fletcher. "I understand the nugget is very valuable."

"I'm glad to hear it. You're a judge. I have an idee of that sort myself."

"About how much does it weigh?"

"About seventy-five pounds. I don't mind gratifying your innocent curiosity, Fletcher."

Fletcher's eyes sparkled.

"It must be very valuable," he said.

"I reckon it is."

"At what do you estimate it—twenty thousand dollars?"

"Not as much as that."

"It ought to come pretty near it, though."

Obed did not answer.

"It's a great prize. You were very lucky."

"So I thought at the time. I don't feel so certain, now," said Obed dryly.

"I think half of it will be enough for you."

"What do you mean, Fletcher?"

"I mean that we shall want half of it."

"How are you going to get it?"

"We mean to hold you prisoner till half the proceeds are brought in from Melbourne."

Obed's countenance fell. He had not thought of this.

Colson's eyes glistened with pleasure. Till that lucky suggestion was made he saw no way of securing a share of the great prize.

"That's a nice scheme, Fletcher," said Obed, regaining his composure.

"So I think. You and the boys would still have a good sum of money. What do you say? Shall we make a little friendly arrangement to that effect? You could give me an order for half the sum realised, and on my securing it you would be released."

"I shall have to talk it over with my partners here," returned Obed. "They're equally interested with me."

"Better do so now."

"I won't till evenin', when we have more time."

Fletcher rode away under the impression that Obed was favourably disposed to his plan.

"When I get the money," he said to himself, "I can decide whether to let the fellow go or not. I don't care for the boys, but I'd like to give this Yankee a good flogging, he's so confoundedly sarcastic. Plague take it, the fellow doesn't know when he's down, but talks as if he was on equal terms with me."

Meanwhile, though Fletcher did not know it, the train of bushrangers had steadily advanced to the neighbourhood of the place where the government escort were encamped.

In fact, he was ignorant that they were so near. But Obed knew it, and he was watching his opportunity to apprise his friends of his situation. Harry had noticed the same thing. Lest he should make a premature revelation, Obed placed his hand to his lips, as a sign of silence. Harry understood, and seemed indifferent, but his heart was beating fast with excitement.

It was certainly an oversight in Fletcher not to have ascertained the situation of the government encampment. He was under the impression that it was in a direction opposite to that in which they were moving, and this determined his course. He was therefore wholly unconscious of danger, and tranquil in mind, though his situation was critical.

Obed was puzzled to know in what manner to get the necessary intelligence to his comrades. Chance gave him a suggestion. The man next him wore round his neck a whistle—designed doubtless to use in case of emergencies. It was of rather peculiar shape.

"That's an odd whistle you've got there, my friend," he said; "where did you get it?"

"In Melbourne," answered the fellow unsuspiciously.

"I think I've seen one like it in the States. Let me look at it a minute."

The bushranger allowed Obed to take it in his hand.

Suddenly Mr. Stackpole put it to his mouth, and gave a sharp, loud whistle that awakened the echoes in the forest.

Like a flash Fletcher turned from his place at the head of the train and eyed the bushranger with a frown. Obed had dropped the whistle, and was walking on with an innocent look.

"What is this foolery, Hogan?" demanded Fletcher sharply. "Don't you know better than to whistle?"

"I didn't, lieutenant," answered Hogan. "It was this man here."

"The Yankee?"

"Yes."

"How did he get the whistle?"

"He asked to look at it."

"What does this mean, Stackpole?" asked Fletcher angrily.

"Don't get riled, squire," said Obed imperturbably. "I just wanted to try it, that's all. I had a whistle once a little like it. When I was workin' for old Deacon Plummer in New Hampshire——"

"I will overlook it this time, but if you take any such liberty again, I'll have you tied to a tree and whipped."

"That's better than bein' shot, anyway. I won't do it again, squire. I ain't particularly anxious to get into trouble."

"These Yankees are about as stupid and presuming as any people I ever met," Fletcher remarked to the comrade who rode beside him. "That fellow is a nuisance, but I mean to teach him a lesson before twenty-four hours are over."

Obed and the two boys awaited with anxiety the result of the summons. The camp was but an eighth of a mile away, but hidden by the trees.

"Will they hear it?" thought Obed.

It is doubtful whether this would have been the case, but luckily for our three friends one of the escort—by name Warner—was taking a walk in the woods, and heard the whistle. His curiosity was excited, and peering through the trees he saw the bushrangers and their captives.

He was a man of promptness, and returning to the camp with all expedition made a report to the officer in command.

"How many are there in the band?" inquired Captain Forbush.

Warner reported.

The captain immediately started, under Warner's guidance, with ten men, and arranged to intercept the bushrangers.

The first intimation Fletcher had of his danger was the sudden appearance of the soldiers, who broke through the underbrush and took the astonished bushrangers in the flank.

"Surrender instantly, or you are dead men!" exclaimed Forbush sternly.

Fletcher fell back in dismay, and was at first speechless with consternation.

"Do you surrender?" repeated the government officer impatiently.

Fletcher's eye ran over the party that confronted him. They outnumbered his own forces two to one. He felt that resistance would be useless.

"We will release our captives if you let us go," he said.

"So you would make conditions? You are in no condition to do that. We propose to free your captives, and to take you to our camp."

"You had better not," said Fletcher, hoping to intimidate the officer. "Our main band is close at hand, and they will avenge us."

"I'll take the risk," said Forbush indifferently. "Throw down your arms!"

As this order was given with each of the bushrangers covered by the weapons of his own party, the bushrangers found it prudent to comply.

"Very well; now follow me."

First, however, the rifles surrendered by the bushrangers were gathered up, and in their defenceless condition they were marched to the government camp. It added to Fletcher's annoyance that the weapons dropped by his party were picked up and carried by their late captives, Obed and the two boys.

"So you're comin' to make us a visit, Fletcher?" said Obed, with an exasperating smile. "It's just as well as if we had gone home with you. We shall be together anyway, and I know you value our society."

"I'd like to strangle you," muttered Fletcher.

"Thank you, but I don't think I should enjoy it. I've seldom met a kinder-hearted man, Fletcher, but you have queer ways of showing it."

Probably the most discomfited members of the party were Colson and Ropes. All their schemes had miscarried, and they felt that they were in a genuine scrape. If they could only convince the officers that they were innocent companions of the bushrangers, they might yet escape. Accordingly, when they reached the camp Colson advanced to Captain Forbush and said: "Ahem! captain, my friend Ropes and I wish to express our thanks to you for your timely rescue, and would like to travel under your escort to Melbourne."

"What does the man mean?" asked Forbush, turning to Obed.

"Suppose you ask him," suggested Obed, with a smile of enjoyment.

"Like your friends here we were captured, but a little earlier. I hope—ha, ha!—you don't take us for bushrangers? That would be a great joke, eh, Ropes?"

"Just so," answered Ropes.

"Suppose you ask Fletcher," again suggested Obed.

"Are these men followers of yours, Mr. Fletcher? They say you captured them."

"They did, did they?" returned Fletcher, eyeing the two men in a manner by no means friendly. "It is a lie. They came to me and reported that your party were carrying a nugget to Melbourne, and wanted us to attack you, and get possession of it. In that case they demanded a share of the proceeds. The dogs! so they want to get favour at our expense, do they?"

"Do you know anything about them, Mr. Stackpole?" asked Captain Forbush.

"Yes, captain, and I am convinced that my friend Fletcher tells the exact truth. That skunk there [indicating Colson] tried to steal the nugget the very night of its discovery, and broke into my cabin for the purpose. He's a sly, underhand thief, and not to be compared with a bold bushranger. I respect them for their pluck at any rate."

"Don't believe him! He's prejudiced against us," whined Colson.

"Gentlemen," said Captain Forbush, "I will comply with your request and allow you to travel with me to Melbourne—under guard!"

Fletcher and the bushrangers looked pleased at this announcement. Their own prospects were not very bright, but they were glad to find that Colson and Ropes were to share their fate.

CHAPTER XVII
FAREWELL TO MELBOURNE

O further adventures or dangers befell the party on their way to Melbourne. It was thought possible that Captain Ring, in charge of the main body of the bushrangers, might attempt a rescue of his companions. No such attack took place. It might have been that he feared the issue of the conflict, but it is also possible that he experienced no poignant regret at the capture of Fletcher, who, he well knew, would have been glad to succeed him in command.

At first Fletcher was buoyed up by the hope of a rescue. Then, when that hope faded out, he sought for an opportunity to escape. In one case he would have succeeded but for the vigilance of Obed Stackpole. The latter, awakening suddenly, saw Fletcher, who in some way had got out of his fetters, stealing quietly away. He sprang to his feet and intercepted the fugitive.

"What, Fletcher! you don't mean to say you are goin' to leave us without sayin' good-bye? We can't spare you, really."

Fletcher tried to shake himself free from the Yankee's detaining grasp.

"Let me alone, you scarecrow!" he exclaimed fiercely.

"Thank you for the compliment, Fletcher," said Obed. "I ain't so han'some as you are, that's a fact, but I guess I'm a good deal better."

As he spoke his grip became stronger, and Fletcher found his efforts to escape absolutely futile.

"I should like to choke you," he said fiercely.

"I've no doubt you would, Fletcher. It would be a nice amusement for you, but I'm not quite ready for the operation just yet. When I am I'll let you know."

"But for you, I would have got away," said Fletcher, in bitter disappointment.

"I guess you would. It's lucky I opened my eyes in time. There'd have been mournin' in this camp if you'd got away, Fletcher. You're wastin' yourself in the woods. You're fitted to adorn Melbourne society, and it won't be my fault if you don't arrive there."

At that moment Captain Forbush awoke.

"What's happened?" he asked anxiously.

"One of our friends was takin' French leave, that's all," said Obed. "I woke just in time to persuade him to stay a little longer."

"Ha! so Fletcher was trying to escape, was he? I am indebted to you, Mr. Stackpole, for frustrating his plan. We can't spare him at all events. I would rather lose any two of his companions."

"You see, Fletcher, how much we value your society," said Obed. "It was cruel in you to leave us."

"You're a fool!" exclaimed Fletcher, darting a look of hate at Obed.

"You never did appreciate me, Fletcher. All I want is your good."

Fletcher was secured in such a way that escape was no longer possible. In due time he and his comrades reached Melbourne as captives, and were transferred to the civil authorities. It may be well to add here that they were tried, and sentenced to a prolonged term of imprisonment. Colson and Ropes fared a little better, their term being only half as long. They submitted sullenly to their fate, but singularly seemed more embittered against Obed Stackpole than against any of the officers through whose hands they passed. Obed would have fared badly had he fallen unprotected into their hands.

It was a joyful day for our young hero, as well as his two companions, when they saw rising before them the roofs and spires of Melbourne. During the weeks that had elapsed since their departure, they had not only "roughed it," but they had met with a series of adventures which were pleasanter to remember than to pass through. Twice they had been captives, but each time they had been providentially rescued. Harry felt that God had watched over him, and delivered him from danger and the schemes of wicked men, and his confidence and trust in an Overruling Power were stronger than ever.

It was some days before they secured the money resulting from the disposal of the nugget. When the matter was finally arranged, they found themselves in possession of about four thousand pounds. This included the sum realised from the sale of the mining claim.

"That gives us about one thousand pounds apiece," said Harry, after a brief calculation.

"I can't believe it," said Jack, who really seemed bewildered by his good fortune. "Why, it's wonderful!"

"So it is, Jack. I dare say you are the richest young sailor of your age in the world."

"When does the next steamer start, Obed?"

"In four days. Can you be ready in that time?"

"I would get ready to start to-morrow if necessary."

"So would I. Melbourne is a nice city, but I'd rather be on dad's farm eatin' supper in the old kitchen than in the best hotel here."

"After all, there's no place like home, Obed."

"That's a fact, but perhaps Jack doesn't feel so."

"My home isn't what it was once," said Jack soberly. "If mother hadn't married again it would have been different, but I never can like or respect my stepfather."

"There's one place you ought to visit before you start for home, Harry," suggested Obed.

"I mean to see the city pretty thoroughly before I go, as I don't imagine I shall ever come this way again."

"That's all right, but it isn't what I mean."

"What then?"

"Do you remember the old gentleman you saved from a ruffian the night before you started for the mines?"

"Mr. Woolson, yes."

"You ought to call, you and Jack."

"I'll go this morning. Will you come too, Jack?"

"I'll go with you anywhere, Harry," said the young sailor, whose affection and admiration for Harry were very strong.

About ten o'clock the boys entered the office of Mr. Woolson. It was situated in one of the handsomest blocks in Little Collins Street, and they learned that he was a wholesale merchant and importer.

"Is Mr. Woolson in?" Harry asked of a clerk.

"He is in the inner office. Have you business with him?"

"Yes."

Admitted into the inner office, the boys saw the old gentleman seated at a large desk with a pile of papers and letters before him. They were by no means certain that he would recognise them, but he did so instantly.

"I am glad to see you, my young friends," he said, rising and shaking hands with them. "I have thought of you often, and of the great service you did me. Have you just returned from the mines?"

"Yes, sir."

"I hope you have had good luck."

"Wonderful luck. Jack and I are worth over a thousand pounds apiece."

"Bless my soul! Why, it only seems a week since you went away."

"It is nearly three months, and seems longer to us, for we have passed through a great deal."

"I shall be glad to hear a full account, but I have not time in business hours. Will you dine with me at my house to-night and spend the evening?"

"With pleasure, sir."

"Then I shall expect you at six o'clock sharp."

The boys met the engagement, and passed the time most agreeably. Jack felt a little bashful, for Mr. Woolson lived in fine style, and Jack was not used to an elegant house or table.

When the cloth was removed, Mr. Woolson asked the boys their plans.

"We intend to sail for home next Saturday," said Harry. "That is as far as we have got."

"If you were willing to stay in Melbourne, I would give you a place in my counting-house."

"Thank you, sir, but I prefer to return home."

"Then I will give you a letter to my nephew and business correspondent. He will further any business views you may have."

"Thank you, sir."

"And I will do the same for your friend, if he desires."

"Thank you, sir," said Jack, "but I mean to keep on as a sailor; I hope some day to be a captain."

"Then I will give you a place on one of our ships, and you shall be promoted as rapidly as you are qualified to rise."

Jack looked gratified, for he knew the value of so powerful a friend.

Late in the evening the boys took leave of the hospitable merchant, and three days afterward they embarked.

We will now return to America, and for the benefit of those readers who are not familiar with Harry's early adventures, as narrated in the story of "Facing the World," I will give a brief account of his story before setting out on the voyage to Australia.

Left an orphan, with a scanty patrimony amounting to three hundred dollars, Harry left it all in the hands of his father's friend, Mr. Benjamin Howard of Ferguson, and set out, not in quest of a fortune, but of a livelihood. He had been recommended by his father to seek a cousin of his, John Fox of Colebrook, and place himself under his guardianship. He visited Mr. Fox, but found him so mean and grasping that he left him after a brief stay, preparing to face the world without assistance. Mr. Fox, who had two children, Joel and Sally, was greatly disappointed, as he had hoped to get control of the boy's slender property, and convert it to his own use. He pursued Harry, but was unable to overtake and capture him.

Months passed, and John Fox heard nothing of his wandering relative.

One day, however, he came home triumphant.

"Well, Maria," he said, addressing his wife, "I've heard of Harry Vane."

"You don't say!" ejaculated Joel, his face screwed up into an expression of curiosity. "What did you hear? Where is he?"

"Joel," answered his father, with an attempt at solemnity, "the judgments of the Lord have fallen upon your unhappy cousin."

"What do you mean, Mr. Fox?" asked his wife, showing curiosity in turn.

"I mean that he is lying dead at the bottom of the sea."

"Don't be so tantalising, Mr. Fox. If you know anything about the boy, out with it!"

When Mrs. Fox spoke in this tone her husband knew that she would not stand any nonsense. So he answered without delay. "Soon after he left our happy home, Maria, he shipped on board the *Nantucket*, as a common sailor, I presume, and the ship was lost off in the Southern Ocean with all on board."

"How awful, pa," said Sally, who alone of all the family had felt kindly toward Harry, "and he was so good-looking, too!"

"He wasn't a bit better-looking than Joel," said her mother sharply.

"Oh, ma!"

"It's true. I never could see any good looks in him, and it doesn't become you, miss, to go against your own brother. How did you find it out, Mr. Fox?"

"I came across an old copy of the *New York Herald*, giving an account of the disaster, and mentioning Harry Vane as one of the passengers. Of course it's a mistake, for he must have been one of the common sailors."

"Well, I reckon there's no call for us to put on mourning," said Mrs. Fox.

"I don't know about that. It might look better."

"What do we care about Harry Vane?"

"My dear, he left property," said Mr. Fox significantly. "There's three hundred dollars in the hands of that man in Ferguson, besides the money he got for saving the train, as much as two hundred dollars. As we are his only relatives, that money ought to come to us by rights."

"That's so, husband. On the whole, I'll put a black ribbon on my bonnet."

"And I'll wear a black necktie," said Joel. "How much of the money am I to have?"

"Wait till we get it," said his father shortly.

"What steps do you propose to take in this matter, Mr. Fox?" queried his wife.

"I'm going to Ferguson to-morrow to see Mr. Benjamin Howard. Of course he won't want to give up the money, but I'll show him I mean business, and am not to be trifled with."

"That's right, pa," said Joel approvingly.

"Five hundred dollars will give us quite a lift," said Mrs. Fox thoughtfully.

"So it will, so it will, my dear. Of course, I'm sorry to hear of the poor boy's death, but I shall insist upon my rights, all the same."

Mrs. Fox warmly approved of her husband's determination, being quite as mean and money-loving as he.

CHAPTER XVIII
A HEART-BROKEN RELATIVE

ATE in the afternoon, John Fox knocked at the door of Benjamin Howard, in the town of Ferguson. It was a hundred miles distant from Colebrook, his own residence, and he grudged the three dollars he had spent for railroad fare; still he thought that the stake was worth playing for.

"I am John Fox of Colebrook," he said, when Mr. Howard entered the room. "You may have heard of me."

"I have," answered Mr. Howard, slightly smiling.

"I am the only living relative of Harry Vane, that is, I and my family."

"I have heard Harry speak of you," said Mr. Howard, non-committally.

"Yes, poor boy! I wish he were alive;" and Mr. Fox drew out a red bandanna handkerchief and covered his eyes, in which there were no tears.

"What do you mean?" asked Mr. Howard, startled.

"Then you haven't heard?"

"Heard—what?"

"That he sailed in the ship *Nantucket*, which was lost, with all on board, in the Southern Ocean?"

It so happened that Mr. Howard had received a letter from Harry after his arrival in Australia, and so knew that Harry was not lost. For a moment he thought Mr. Fox might have later information, but saw that it was not so. He decided to draw Mr. Fox on, and ascertain his object in calling.

"I hope that this is not so," he said gravely.

"There is not a doubt of it," answered Fox. "There's an account of the loss of the vessel in the *New York Herald*. I cut it out, and have it in my pocket-book. Would you like to see it?"

"If you please."

Mr. Fox produced the scrap, and asked triumphantly, "Doesn't that settle it?"

"Suppose that it does, what then?"

"What then? It follows that Harry's money comes to me and my family, as the only surviving relatives. You've got money of his, the boy told me."

"Yes."

"About how much?"

"About three hundred dollars."

"So I thought. That money ought to be handed over to me."

"I don't see that, Mr. Fox."

"You don't see that?" interrogated Fox sharply. "Do you mean to keep it yourself?"

"Not for my own use; I am not that kind of a man, Mr. Fox. But I have no authority to hand the money over in the unceremonious way you expect."

"Why not? Isn't the boy dead?"

"I have no proof of it."

"What better proof do you want than the *New York Herald*?"

"The account in the *Herald* may contain errors."

"Perhaps you think the boy could swim to shore a few hundred miles," suggested John Fox with sarcasm.

"No, I don't think that likely."

"Then what possible chance had he to escape?"

"He might have been rescued by a passing vessel."

"Look here, Mr. Howard," said Fox indignantly, "you don't mean what you say. You evidently mean to keep that money from the lawful claimants. I am not much surprised. I expected it. But I can tell you here and now that John Fox isn't a man to be cheated and imposed upon. I mean to have my rights."

"Are you aware, Mr. Fox, that your language is offensive and insulting?"

"I don't care. I came here for justice. That money ought not to be in your hands, who are no kith nor kin to Harry Vane. It ought to go to me, and I mean to sue you for it."

"Mr. Fox, I propose to obey the law, but it appears to me that you are taking it for granted that Harry Vane is dead without sufficient proof."

"What more proof do you want than this paragraph? The fact is, you don't want to believe it."

"No!" answered Mr. Howard in a tone of emotion, "I don't want to believe that poor Harry is dead."

"Nor I," said John Fox. "If the boy hadn't been foolish and left my happy home, he'd have been alive to-day. But we can't alter facts. He's dead, and all our grief won't bring him back."

Benjamin Howard looked at the man curiously. "His grief doesn't seem to be very profound," he thought. "I will test him."

"Even if I were convinced that poor Harry was dead," he said, "I should not deliver up the money till you had established a legal claim to it."

"So you mean to put all possible obstacles in my way," said John Fox, provoked. "I thought so. But, Mr. Howard, let me tell you that you can't rob the orphan."

"Meaning yourself?"

"No, I mean the dead boy—that is the orphan's estate—without settling with *me*. I am a man of influence, I'd have you know, and I'll put the matter in the hands of the lawyer right off."

"It might be well, first, to listen to what I have to say."

"Aha! he's scared!" thought John Fox.

"I'm ready to hear what you've got to say," he answered, "but it won't influence me a particle."

"I think it will. Harry Vane is alive!"

"What!" ejaculated John Fox, his face expressing his dismay. "It's a lie. I don't believe it."

"Georgie," said Mr. Howard to his little son, who just then entered the room, "go to my desk and bring me Harry Vane's letter."

This was done at once, John Fox meanwhile sitting in painful suspense.

"This letter," said Mr. Howard, taking it in his hand, "was posted, as you see, at Melbourne, Australia. Harry was shipwrecked on an island, from which he finally escaped, and was carried to Melbourne. He writes me that he has gone to the mines, and is hoping to find some gold there."

"Is this true?" asked Fox, in a hollow voice.

"I will read you the letter, and show you the signature."

"I think it's a forgery."

"No chance of that. I know Harry Vane's handwriting well. But you don't look well, Mr. Fox. I thought you would be pleased to hear that Harry had escaped from the perils of shipwreck and is alive."

John Fox did not reply, but after examining the letter he rose with a rueful countenance, and departed unceremoniously, a badly disappointed man.

"It'll cost me three dollars to get back," he groaned, "and I shall have to stop at a hotel, for there is no train till to-morrow. 'Most ten dollars gone altogether—just thrown away! I'm a very unlucky man."

The news he carried home brought grief to Mrs. Fox and Joel. Only Sally seemed glad that Harry was still living. For so expressing herself she was severely rebuked by her mother.

CHAPTER XIX
HOME AGAIN

T was a bright, beautiful morning when our three friends landed in New York. Their voyage had been a favourable one, and they had made some pleasant acquaintances, but they were overjoyed to tread once more the familiar streets and see the familiar sights of the American metropolis.

They registered at a quiet hotel on the European system, intending to remain in the city a few days. They sought out a prominent broker and asked his advice about the investment of their money. He received them in a friendly manner, and gave them the best advice in his power. Each reserved three hundred dollars for present use.

It was a novelty to all of them to be free from anxiety on the score of money, and it may well be believed that all enjoyed the feeling.

The second morning, as they were walking down Broadway, their eyes fell upon a familiar figure. Directly in front of them they beheld a slender young man, dressed in the extreme of fashion, swinging a light cane. As he walked along it was easy to see that he was on the most comfortable and agreeable terms with himself, and firmly persuaded that he was an object of general admiration.

"Montgomery Clinton!" exclaimed Harry and Jack simultaneously.

"You don't mean to say you know that critter!" said Obed, eyeing Mr. Clinton with evident curiosity.

"Yes, he was one of the *Nantucket* passengers, and shipwrecked with us," said Harry. "He did not remain in Australia, but took a return vessel at once."

"That was lucky. A critter like that wouldn't be of much account at the mines."

"Stop! I am going to speak to him."

Harry quickened his step, and touched Mr. Clinton on the shoulder.

Clinton turned languidly, but when he saw who it was his face expressed undisguised pleasure.

"Mr. Vane!" he exclaimed. "I'm awfully glad to see you, don't you know?"

"You haven't forgotten my friend Jack, I hope," said Harry, indicating the young sailor.

"I am glad to see him, too," said Mr. Clinton, with modified pleasure, offering two fingers for Jack to shake, for he had not forgotten that Jack had been a sailor.

"When did you come from Australia?" asked Clinton.

"We only arrived day before yesterday."

"And what luck did you have at the mines?"

"We struck it rich. We are all capitalists, Jack and all."

"You don't say so! I wish I had gone with you, really now."

"I don't think you'd have liked it, Mr. Clinton. We had a hard time. We had to wade through mud and mire, and sleep on the ground, and twice we were captured by bushrangers. They wanted Jack and myself to join the band."

"You don't say so—really?"

"They might have made you a bushranger, Mr. Clinton, if they had caught you."

"I never would consent, never!" said Mr. Clinton, with emphasis.

Jack smiled at the idea of the elegant Mr. Clinton being transformed into an outlaw and bushranger.

"I am awfully glad I did not go with you," he said, shuddering.

"Let me make you acquainted with my friend, Mr. Obed Stackpole, Mr. Clinton," said Harry. "He was with us in all our trials and dangers."

Montgomery Clinton surveyed Obed with evident curiosity. The long gaunt figure of the Yankee was clad in a loose rough suit which was too large for him, and Clinton shuddered at the barbarous way in which he was attired.

"Glad to make your acquaintance, Mr. Stickpole," he said politely.

"*Stack*pole, if it's all the same to you, friend Clinton," corrected Obed. "Glad to see any friend of Harry's and Jack's. You look as if you had just come out of a bandbox."

"Oh, thank you," said the gratified dude. "You're awfully kind. My friends think I have a little taste in dress."

"My friends never paid me that compliment," said Obed. "Say, how do you like my fit out?"

"I—I don't think they have very good tailors in Australia," said Clinton hesitatingly.

"Have you as many pairs of trousers as ever, Mr. Clinton?" asked Harry.

"I have only nineteen, Mr. Vane, but I shall order some more soon."

"Nineteen pairs of breeches!" ejaculated Obed in amazement. "What in the name of Jehoshaphat do you want of so many?"

"Well, I don't want to have people get used to seeing me in the same trousers, don't you know, so every day I wear a different pair."

"It must cost a mint of money to buy so many clothes."

"Oh, I have accounts with four or five tailors. They're willing to wait, don't you know. They appreciate a gentleman's custom."

"How long do they wait?" asked Harry.

"I'm owing some two years. There's lots of fellows make them wait as long."

"That ain't my way," said Obed. "I pay cash. Don't they make a fuss?"

"Oh, they send in their bills, but I don't take any notice of them," said Clinton languidly.

"Then, young man," said Obed, "let me advise you to pay your bills, and get back your self-respect. I'd go six months with only a pair of breeches, sooner than cheat a tailor out of a new pair."

"I never wear breeches," drawled Clinton, with a shudder. "I don't know what they are. Mr. Vane, those trousers you have on are very unbecoming. Let me introduce you to my tailor. He'll fit you out in fashionable style."

"Thank you. I believe I do need a new pair."

"Will he fit me, too?" asked Obed.

"He don't make—breeches!" said Clinton disdainfully.

"A good hit, by Jehoshaphat!" exclaimed Obed, slapping Clinton on the back with such emphasis that he was nearly upset.

"Don't hit quite so hard," said the dude ruefully. "You nearly upset me, don't you know?"

"I know it now. The fact is, friend Clinton, you ought to be shut up in a glass case, and put on exhibition in a dime museum."

"How awfully horrid!" protested Clinton.

"You're more fit for ornament than use."

"You're awfully sarcastic, Mr. Stickpole, don't you know?" said Clinton, edging off cautiously. "I must bid you good morning, Mr. Vane, as I have to buy a new necktie. I will go to the tailor's any day."

"What was such a critter made for, anyway?" queried Obed, when Clinton was out of hearing. "He looks for all the world like a tailor's dummy."

CHAPTER XX
THE BOYS SECURE POSITIONS

EFORE leaving New York, Harry Vane decided to call upon the nephew to whom Mr. Woolson of Melbourne had given him a letter of introduction. Upon inquiry, he found that John Woolson & Co. (the style of the firm) were large importers in the lower part of the city.

Accompanied by Jack, he called one morning Mr. John Woolson, a courteous gentleman, about forty years of age, received him with politeness, which changed to cordiality when he had read his uncle's letter.

"My uncle writes here that you two young gentlemen recently rendered him an important service."

"We were fortunate enough to save him from being robbed," said Harry modestly.

"And maltreated, also, I presume," said the nephew. "When did you arrive in New York?"

"Last Thursday, sir."

"Did you leave my uncle well?"

"He looked in excellent health."

"How long do you remain in the city? What are your plans?"

"We think of leaving to-morrow. We wish to see friends from whom we have long been parted."

"My uncle wishes me to offer you a position in my establishment, Mr. Vane. If that will meet your views, I shall be happy to receive you."

"I should like nothing better, sir," replied Harry, his eyes sparkling.

"Will fifteen dollars a week satisfy you to begin with."

"But, sir, I can't hope to earn as much as that."

"Well, perhaps not just at first," said the merchant, smiling; "but if your looks don't belie you, it will not be long before your services will be worth that sum. At any rate I am ready to pay it."

"Thank you, sir," said Harry gratefully. "When would you wish me to commence?"

"When you please. You had better take a vacation of a month to visit your friends. Then come to the city, and enter my employment."

Harry renewed his thanks, and Mr. Woolson turned to Jack.

"You have been trained as a sailor, I believe," he said.

"Yes, sir."

"Do you wish to follow the sea?"

"Yes, sir," answered Jack promptly. "I love the sea."

"Then I will find you a good position on one of my ships, commend you specially to the captain as a young friend of mine, and promote you as fast as your progress in seamanship will warrant my doing so."

Now it was Jack's turn to look jubilant, for nothing could have suited him better.

"You too will want a vacation. Take as long as you like, and then come to me. By the way, I don't know how you are situated as regards money. If either of you desires an advance, I shall be glad to accommodate you."

"We met with good luck at the mines," said Harry "and are both well supplied with money. We thank you, however, for your kind offer."

The boys left the office in high spirits.

"I don't see but our prospects are bright, Jack," said Harry.

"I didn't think so when we were on the island," said Jack, "or when we were captives among the bushrangers."

"No; we have certainly seen some hard times. Let us hope that we have had our share, and may look forward now to happier days."

Now that their future was arranged, the boys were in a hurry to leave the city and visit their friends. Obed sympathised with them.

"Boys," said he, "I'm gettin' kinder homesick. There's an old man and a girl I want to see, and tell 'em of my good luck."

"Your father and——"

"Suke Stanwood. Suke has been waitin' for me five years, and there ain't no need of waitin' any longer. If all goes well she'll be Mrs. Obed Stackpole within a month."

"She may not be able to get her wedding things so soon, Obed."

"She don't need any wedding things. Any dress'll do to be married in."

"You will send us some cards and cake, I hope, Obed."

"Better'n that: I'll send you an invite to the weddin'."

"Then it'll have to come soon, Obed. I shall be gone to the city, and Jack to sea within a month."

"Then we'll hurry it up. It'll give me a good excuse. But there's one thing I'm going to do before I get married."

"What is that?"

"Pay off the mortgage on dad's farm. It's only a thousand dollars, but dad couldn't lift it if he lived to a hundred."

"And what are you going to do, Obed?"

"There's a farm alongside I can buy for twenty-five hundred dollars, with a comfortable house thrown in. I can buy it, and have more than enough money left to furnish the house and stock the farm."

"I wish you happiness, Obed; but don't you think you'll ever pine to be back in Australia?"

"I may hanker after a sight of Fletcher and his two cronies, Colson and Ropes," returned Obed with dry humour, "but we can't have everything in this world, and I'll try to rub along with the blessings I have."

Let me add here that Obed carried out his programme. He paid the mortgage, bought the farm, and in less than three weeks he was a married man. Harry and Jack were at the wedding, and received great attention from all Obed's friends. To the inhabitants of the little village it seemed wonderful that boys so young should have travelled so far, and passed through such varied experiences.

"I expect an invite to each of your weddings, boys," said Obed, as they were on the point of leaving him. "One good turn deserves another."

"You will have to exercise a little patience, Obed," said Harry, smiling.

"Don't wait as long as I did," said Obed. "I got to be a cranky old bachelor before I hitched horses."

"Mrs. Stackpole will soon cure you of that," said Harry, with a smile.

CHAPTER XXI
CONCLUSION

HEN Harry had completed his business in New York, he took the train at once to his native village. His arrival made quite a sensation. Not only Mr. Howard, his father's friend, received him with joy, but there were many other friends besides who rejoiced in his good fortune.

"You have been very fortunate, Harry," said Mr. Howard. "You tell me that you have about five thousand dollars?"

"Yes, sir, and it makes me feel rich."

"Besides the two thousand dollars I have in charge for you."

"Two thousand dollars!" ejaculated Harry in amazement. "You mean three hundred, Mr. Howard."

"No, I mean what I say," replied his friend, with a smile.

"But I don't understand——"

"Don't you remember the fifty shares of mining stock you placed in my hands?"

"Yes, they were given me by my father. I thought them worthless."

"A month ago I learned the contrary. I took the liberty, without consulting you, as you were absent, to sell them. They realised seventeen hundred dollars net, thus carrying up the amount in my hands to two thousand dollars."

"Is it possible that I am worth seven thousand dollars? It seems wonderful!"

"But the best of it is that it is true. Then was there not a sum of money which you received for saving a railroad train?"

"Yes, I have used part of it, but one hundred and fifty dollars remain. It is in the hands of a Mr. Conway, president of the road."

"Then it appears to me, Harry, taken in connection with your offer of employment in New York, you are in a very enviable position. How old are you?"

"I shall soon be seventeen."

"Then you are beginning the world young. Continue to deserve good fortune, and you are likely to prosper."

Before returning to New York Harry felt inclined to visit his would-be guardian, John Fox, whose treatment of him has been recorded at length in "Facing the World."

He took the train, as before, to Bolton, and thence went by stage to Colebrook. He walked to the Fox mansion, and going up to the front door knocked.

The door was opened by Mrs. Fox herself. She did not immediately recognise Harry in his handsome suit, with a gold chain crossing his vest, attached, it may be added, to a handsome gold watch, which he had bought in New York.

"What is your business, young man?" she asked.

"Don't you remember me, Mrs. Fox?" asked Harry.

"Land's sake! It ain't Harry Vane!" she exclaimed in wonder.

"Yes, it is," answered Harry, smiling. "I hope Mr. Fox and Joel are well."

"Come in, and I'll call Joel. You've been doing well, ain't you?" she asked, surveying him with eager curiosity.

"I have been very fortunate indeed."

"I thought you was drowned—wrecked on a ship or something."

"If I was, I have come to life again."

"Well, well, it's strange. I'll call Joel."

Joel, who was at the barn, soon entered. He, too, surveyed Harry curiously.

"How d'y'do?" he said. "I never expected to set eyes on you again. Is that a gold watch you have?"

"Yes, Joel."

"Let me see it. How much did it cost?"

"A hundred dollars, besides the chain."

"Gosh! Ain't that a sight of money! Did you spend all your money on it?"

"No, I bought a chain too."

"To my mind you was very foolish to spend all your hard earnin's that way! There's no fool like a young fool," said Mrs. Fox severely.

"But, Mrs. Fox, I have some money left."

"How much?" asked Joel eagerly.

"Seven thousand dollars."

"Gosh all Jerusalem! you ain't yarnin', be you? Seven thousand dollars!"

"Who's talkin' of seven thousand dollars?" asked a familiar voice, as Mr. Fox entered the room.

"Harry Vane says he's worth seven thousand dollars!" exclaimed Joel, in a tone made up of amazement, jealousy, and wonder.

"Is that true?" asked John Fox, in equal amazement.

"Yes, Mr. Fox."

"But how on 'arth——"

Then Harry gave a full explanation, with which I don't propose to trouble the reader, as it would be a twice-told tale.

"Some folks seem born to luck!" said Mr. Fox furiously, when Harry had completed his story. "Joel may work and toil all his life, and he won't get no seven thousand dollars. It seems hard!"

John Fox had been much impressed by Harry's luck, and his avaricious soul was busying itself with some scheme for turning it to his personal advantage.

"I'm glad you've been so lucky, Harry," he said, with affected cordiality. "It beats all, I must say. I've no doubt you are ready now to carry out your dear father's dyin' wish."

"What was that, Mr. Fox?"

"He wanted me to be your guardeen. It stands to reason a boy of sixteen ain't to be trusted with so much money. Now I'm an experienced man of business, and I'm willin' to be your guardeen, and I won't charge you a cent for takin' care of your property except board money."

"Thank you, Mr. Fox," said Harry, with an amused smile, "but I am offered a place in New York at fifteen dollars a week, and I have friends who will advise me about the investment of my money."

"Fifteen dollars a week!" repeated Mr. Fox dolefully. "Can't you get a place for Joel in the same store?"

"If I can find Joel a satisfactory place in the city I will do so," said Harry, "but I ought to say that my employer only pays me high wages out of favour."

"I'll take ten," said Joel eagerly. "You know you and me was always friends, Harry."

"Joel always liked you," said politic Mr. Fox.

Harry knew better, but he was on good terms with the world, and he did not dispute this statement.

"I'll do what I can," he said. "Meanwhile, Mr. Fox, I should like to make Joel and his sister a small present."

He gave them each a ten-dollar bill, which made Joel's eyes sparkle with joy.

Mr. Fox renewed his suggestion that Harry select him as a "guardeen," but Harry politely but firmly declined to entertain the proposal. Nevertheless, when he left the house, he was warmly urged to come again and often. He understood the reason of the cordiality, and knew very well that if he had come back poor his reception would have been very different.

Before going back to New York he made a visit of a couple of days to his old friend and employer, Professor Hemmenway, the prestidigitateur, who was delighted with the success of his young friend. He offered Harry a new engagement, but of course it was declined.

In New York he met Jack, and inquired how he had fared.

"I found my stepfather dying," answered Jack. "In fact he drank himself to death after wasting all mother's property. But I have bought her a small house, and insured her an income sufficient to keep her comfortable. The last will require some of my principal, but I shall be earning good wages, and can make it up when I return home."

"When do you sail, Jack?"

"Next week, on one of Mr. Woolson's ships. I am to go to China."

"I hope you'll steer clear of the island we were wrecked on, Jack."

"I never want to see it again, Harry; still it brought us luck."

"I shall be sorry to part with you, Jack. I wish you could be content to stay in New York."

"No, Harry, I can't give up the sea yet. It is my great ambition to command a ship myself some time."

"I think you will accomplish it, Jack, for you stand well with the owners."

Five years have passed. Harry and Jack are each twenty-one. Harry occupies a confidential position with the firm, and is likely to be a partner before he is much older. Jack is first mate, and will be a captain before he is twenty-five. His mother is living, and happy in his success, and enjoying the comfortable home he has provided for her.

Harry obtained a position for Joel in the city, but he proved unsatisfactory to his employer and was soon discharged. Another situation he held as brief a time. At last he was obliged to go home and assist his father, who treats him almost as penuriously as he would have done Harry. Joel is dissatisfied and unhappy, and his mother thinks he was born to bad luck, but those who know Joel think his want of success springs from a different source. Harry and Jack obtained success because they deserved it. If Joel were more like them he too might succeed. And I am sorry to say he is looking forward impatiently to the time when he shall inherit his father's property. It is very wrong, but perhaps Mr. Fox himself is partly to blame.

Whenever Jack comes home from a voyage he calls upon Harry, and together they talk over their adventures in a new world. Sometimes Obed Stackpole calls also. He has two boys, whom he has named respectively Harry and Jack in honour of his two companions in Australia.

www.ingramcontent.com/pod-product-compliance
Lightning Source LLC
Chambersburg PA
CBHW072155200426
43209CB00052B/1266